ALL

GRACE

CW01467377

ALL
GRACE

*New Teachings from Jesus
on the Truth About Life*

GINA LAKE

Endless Satsang Foundation

www.RadicalHappiness.com

Cover photo: © Subbotina/CanStockPhoto.com

ISBN: 978-1540814395

Copyright © 2017 by Gina Lake

All rights reserved. No part of this book may be used or reproduced by any means, graphic, electronic, or mechanical, including photocopying, recording, taping, or by any information storage retrieval system without the written permission of the publisher except in the case of brief quotations embodied in critical articles and reviews.

To the One in everyone.

CONTENTS

PREFACE

The experience of receiving this book and the others I've received from Jesus is as if Jesus were sitting beside me, dictating these words, except that I hear them internally instead of in the usual way. The words that I hear in my head are distinct from my own thoughts. They have a tonality and feel to them, an energy, representative of the kindness and gentleness of the one we have known as Jesus. This process is called conscious channeling.

Before this book, I received three others from Jesus in a similar way (The Jesus Trilogy, A Heroic Life, and In the World but Not of It) and many others before that from another nonphysical being. These books have required no organizing and only light editing on my part. I have benefited greatly from this process, from both the teachings and the transmission coming through them.

My relationship with Jesus is straightforward and simple. He is a teacher for me, as he is for so many. He is not a personal guide, as that is not his purpose, except in regard to our work together. I have agreed to be his scribe, and when he feels I am ready for the next project, we begin. I never quite know how it will shape up, although I am told ahead of time very generally what it will be about. Writing in this way is a little like driving blind. It requires trust that the words will be given and that there is a point to be made and an organization that will be revealed over time.

Unlike the many books that have been written about the teachings of Jesus, the books I've been given by Jesus are not a study or explanation of the words he spoke two thousand years ago. In these channeled books, Jesus is presenting material that he would present if he were alive today, or so I am told, and they are in today's language.

Of all the books I've brought forth so far, this one is the least related to the early teachings of Jesus. So those who are expecting it to sound as Jesus sounded so long ago might be disappointed or even skeptical. Jesus, himself, explains later in this book that Jesus of Nazareth was but one incarnation of his and that he resides on another dimension, not as this one individual, but as a multi-dimensional being. From that dimension, he continues to use the personage of Jesus to stay in touch with, teach, and guide human beings, especially those devoted to him and his teachings as Jesus.

Having said this, I hope you can set aside any preconceptions and expectations around the one dictating these words and just allow the words to, hopefully, touch your heart and transform your mind. So now, I will step aside to allow you to experience the one who once was Jesus, as he speaks directly to you.

Gina Lake, February, 2017

INTRODUCTION

I, the one you have known as Jesus the Christ, am presenting you with information in this book that is a little different from my previous books. The information is more metaphysical than what you might expect. I am including metaphysical truths along with principles for how to live a better, more loving, and peaceful life on earth.

Some of what I write about here might confuse you or seem "airy-fairy," but I assure you that there are fairies as sure as there is air! So much of the universe is unseen, unknown, and not even imagined by you. By expanding your mind to include more possibilities, your life and its concerns are put into perspective. You are eternal and magnificent, and I am determined to remind you of that. This book is just one of the ways I am doing that. So please open your mind and your heart, and I will begin with three important truths...

Jesus, dictated to Gina Lake
February, 2017

CHAPTER 1

Three Truths

Grace is the movement of Oneness as it manifests and "plays" in this world of duality. Grace is the effect of Oneness on creation, like the wind upon the water. This world and every other world in the infinity that is creation was made manifest as an expression of the Oneness and also provides experience for the Oneness. This Oneness is another word for God or what I have called the Father or, more simply, the intelligence behind and expressing through all life.

Whether you are religious or not, it is likely apparent to you that there is intelligence behind and imbued in life, in fact, an incomprehensible intelligence from your perspective. To capitalize "intelligence" and call it "an Intelligence" may not be acceptable to some and is also not a fair representation, as it implies a particular being, a Supreme Being.

The intelligence I am speaking about is not a being, unless you would describe that being as All That Is or one that encompasses all life within infinity. This infinity cannot be grasped by you, and you have no language to depict it accurately. Since I am limited by your language, I will have to refer to this creative force or intelligence as if it existed separate from you and from creation, while it does not.

This fact, that the Oneness is not separate from you, is also incomprehensible, although mystics have had glimpses of this truth. I say "glimpse," because what mystics have experienced of Oneness is limited by the human body-mind and its capacity to experience Oneness.

If you have had a mystical experience, you may feel that you have experienced God or the truth about life. And yet, it is quite impossible to experience the fullness of this truth while you remain in a body. Even I and others like me, who are no longer physical, have not experienced the fullness of this truth, as this infinite intelligence remains unfathomable even to those further along the evolutionary path than you. And yet, here I am attempting to write about it in a way that will light your path.

You are as dear to Life as life itself. You *are* life, as it is being lived by you, in your unique way. No other experience is exactly like yours. You are meant to bring a unique experience to the Divine, to this mysterious force that is life and has created all life. You are its expression—and not just your current expression. You shift and change throughout the eternity within which you exist and experience an infinite number of unique expressions.

Contemplate this for a moment: your infinite existence. What if you thought of yourself as infinite existence instead of a limited mortal, constrained within a body? What if you knew yourself as infinite existence? Could you suffer? If you realized how very fleeting each of your experiences is, could you suffer?

You suffer because you hold on to experiences that have already passed. You keep them alive by clinging to them through thought. You create stories around them that

perpetuate the suffering. Or you suffer because you believe
something that isn't true about an experience you are having:
"This shouldn't be happening. I'll never be happy. I can't stand
this!"

What if your thoughts, your feelings, and even your
sensations were not personal, that is, what if they didn't appear
to be happening to someone, but just to life? What if you are the
experiencing of life in a particular locality and not the one who
has a story about those experiences? What if life is just life, not
"your life"? That is the truth.

That *you* are experiencing anything is a mirage, because *you*
are a mirage. *You* are not experiencing anything. Life is
experiencing something through the body-mind that seems to
belong to a *you*. There is a body-mind that is a sensing and
experiencing device, but there is actually no *you*, no entity,
sensing and experiencing life, only life experiencing whatever it
seems this imaginary you is experiencing. This brings us to the
first truth about life: *You are life, and you are infinite!*

You are God's experience of the universe in the particular
corner of the universe inhabited by your body-mind. Your
body-mind localizes experience and makes it seem that *you* are
having a particular experience, but you are having this
experience on behalf of God, the Creator. You are the Creator
experiencing life through the particular body-mind that is
attached to the imaginary sense of you.

This sense of being you is just that: a sense, an impression,
an idea. It is built into the body-mind to give the body-mind
and its experiences the illusion that those experiences belong to
somebody rather than to life. This is the great Illusion. The idea
of you existing as something other than God is an illusion. The
truth is, there is only life existing through form: the Formless
expressing through form.

You know what this feels like whenever you simply stop thinking yourself into creation. Your thoughts create the sense of being you. The proof is that when you stop thinking, which is rare for most people, you stop creating this imaginary you, and you lose yourself in the Mystery; you experience the truth about who you really are. But because the experience of the Truth is often uncomfortable, since it is unfamiliar, most people quickly return to creating themselves through thought.

This is fascinating, how you do this! You create yourself by thinking about yourself! But the self you create lives only in your imagination and in other people's imaginations (although quite differently), as they also share in the great Illusion.

Of course, you were designed to do this. The great Illusion is not a mistake but designed to allow the Formless to experience itself as form. The Formless imagines a possible character and *"Voila!"* that imagination is made manifest and takes on a life of its own, thanks to something similar to what you understand as programming.

You are programmed to be as you are because the Creator intends to experience life through such a one as you. Given this, one can only conclude that every creation is equally beloved and appreciated by the Creator, since the Creator made everything to be exactly as it is. Exactly! You are meant to be just as you are and just as you have been and just as you will be.

This is not to say that the Creator knows how you will behave in every circumstance, because as part of your design, you were also endowed with free will, the ability to make choices within the circumstances and abilities you were given. You can't choose to be other than you are or to have talents other than those you have, but you can choose *how* you will be as this character—how you play this character.

This is a lot of freedom, since it determines your experience of being this character: whether you will be happy or not and whether you will have a good life or not as this character. For example, you can be angry, mean, unhappy, violent, selfish, or fearful as this character, or not. It's your choice. Although how you behave may not always seem like a choice, since behavior is so often shaped by conditioning, which can be very compelling, the truth is you do have a choice. You have been given that power.

How you choose to be determines how you will experience life. You don't create everything about your life, just as you don't create your programming (although your soul in conjunction with other forces agrees to that programming). But you do create your *experience* of life by what you choose to believe and how you respond to the conditions in which you find yourself.

No matter what inner experience you create for yourself — sadness, anger, regret, hatred, resentment, blame, victimhood, loneliness — the Divine is willing to have that experience for however long you choose to create that. And when you create a different inner experience, the Divine is willing to have that one. In this way, you learn to take responsibility for your inner state and to create a more positive, loving inner state. Life is so benevolent that you get to choose your inner experience, if you are conscious enough, even if you don't have a choice about what life brings you.

The Divine gives you free will, but it has a will of its own, which sometimes trumps your free will. You don't always get what you want, because life has a higher order and a higher plan within which your existence fits. You are guided by this higher will to fit into the greater plan.

Although you have no control over the greater plan or how you fit into it, you do have some control within your plan: You can do your plan this way or that way. But for the most part, you will fulfill your plan some way. To the extent that your free will is aligned with your plan, you will be happy. To the extent that it isn't, you will be unhappy and experience more difficulties than necessary.

For example, if your plan for this lifetime is to uplift children, there are many ways you might do that: as a mother, a teacher, a child psychologist, or a researcher of child behavior, to name a few possibilities. With this as your plan, you will naturally feel attracted to such roles. How you will specifically fulfill your plan is determined by your free will and circumstances. Your family, the people you meet, where you live, events, available opportunities, and other circumstances will all contribute to shaping the particular role and direction you will take.

If you are fulfilling your plan, you will naturally feel fulfilled. If you aren't, you won't feel fulfilled. In this way, your soul clearly communicates the direction in which to go. Go in the direction of fulfillment and joy, and you can't go wrong.

If for some reason you don't go in that direction, the intelligence behind life, Grace, will attempt to redirect you. If you resist its gentle nudges, Grace prods less gently or sets up roadblocks to continuing in the current direction. It makes your life harder.

Grace eases the way in directions you are meant to go in and interferes with others. Life is very kind this way. It shows you the way with carrots and sticks. But most importantly, Grace gives you an inner compass that tells you which way to go: Follow your joy, your fulfillment, your passion, your love!

Yes, God has a will, and that will is carried out by Grace. But that will is not separate from your will. You actually want what God wants, although you don't always know that. Sometimes you *think* you want something else, but you are mistaken. Then God shows you that by either letting you have what you think you want or by not letting you have it. You are always better off when you want what God wants.

What does God want, and how do you know what that is?

❖ *When God wants you to learn something, God lets you have what you think you want.*

❖ *When God wants you to make a different choice, God doesn't let you have what you think you want.*

When you want what God wants, you are happy. That's how you know that what you are thinking and doing is aligned with God's design for you: You are happy, at peace, and in the flow.

Being in the flow doesn't necessarily feel remarkable or fantastic. Fantastic is an idea about happiness and an over-the-top feeling that is experienced relatively briefly, usually when the ego finally gets what it wants. Being in the flow is so ordinary that you might not even notice you are in the flow, especially since being in the flow, by its nature, involves very little self-reflection.

In the flow, there is no *me* to think about itself. The flow happens in the absence of thought or despite any thoughts that might be present, particularly thoughts about *me*. Since self-reflection is absent or at a minimum, being in the flow feels natural, simple, and problem-free. It is how life can be lived most of the time once you realize one thing: *You are not in*

control of life, and you don't need to be because your infinite self is!
This is another truth about life.

You only *think* you have more control than you do, and
you *want* control. But wanting something doesn't equal having
it—or needing it. You have less control than you think and
more than you need. In other words, you don't have much
control *and* you don't need it.

People are under the illusion that they can control things
they can't actually control. For instance, they think they can
control how healthy they are by what they do for their bodies.
However, your knowledge about the body is so limited that
attempts to determine your health are also limited. So much of
one's health is governed by subconscious processes and genes,
which are not under your control.

A lack of knowledge is not the only thing that stands in the
way of greater control. Perfect knowledge would still not give
you control. In addition to there being a higher will and a
higher plan at work that trumps your own will, the nature of
life is simply too complex to be controlled.

Too many factors are influencing every outcome, most of
which you can never be aware of or affect, for you to be in
control. The few factors you do have control over will never be
enough to be in control. When you seem to be in control, the
factors you are in control of have simply won out over the
others for the time being. Because the mix of factors and their
strength is in constant flux, even when you think you are in
control, or should be, it turns out you aren't. Life is full of
surprises!

This is not intended to discourage you from trying to get
what you want, but only to help you see that you are not to
blame when you don't get what you want. If you think you can
control life and you aren't able to, the conclusion is often that

you failed, that *you* are inadequate. Your failures to control life are taken personally. But more often than not, whatever you wanted was simply not meant to be, for one reason or another. It was not in the cards.

Cards are an excellent metaphor for the complexity and unpredictability of life. However, cards are more random than life, since life has a plan and a guiding hand: Grace. In life, you could say that the cards are rigged in favor of the house.

In life, the factors that create any situation or event are like the cards that get played by the various players involved. Because the players have free will, what card will be played is never known, until it is. Although certain cards are more likely to get played than others, you never know! Many factors influence what cards gets played and if a card gets played. Then whatever card is played determines the next card or cards that are played. The order in which the cards fall is everything. What came before can't help but influence what comes next.

In life, many factors contribute to someone taking a certain action and when, or not acting. Although people have free will, no one has that much control over even their own choices, given the power of conditioning and how easily influenced by others people are. People's choices are determined by both immediate factors, such as their thoughts and feelings and the influences around them, and by less immediate and direct factors going back in time.

The vast array of factors involved in creating any situation are determined by many previous events and countless people with their various conditioning and perceptions, all of which are outside of not only your control but other people's. The causes that shape any situation or event are impossible to pinpoint or enumerate, as essentially everything that ever happened throughout history contributed to the way things are, to the cards falling as they did.

Can you create a certain outcome with your thoughts alone, as so many believe? If something went wrong, could it have been avoided by thinking more positively or by not thinking something? Possibly. But, as just pointed out, one's thoughts are just one factor involved in the creation of reality.

Nevertheless, thoughts definitely create your imaginary reality, your inner experience of reality! Reality seems and feels as you imagine it to be. For example, if you imagine it to be scary, then it seems and feels scary. Or if you imagine it to be good, it seems and feels good. But that doesn't mean that imagining reality the way you would like it to be will make it be that way. That would be fuzzy thinking.

Your thoughts *do* matter; they just aren't responsible for creating all of reality. Thoughts color your *experience* of reality and so also influence your choices and behavior, but thoughts don't singlehandedly create reality. The world is not designed to comply to your thoughts about it. The fact that life occasionally does comply to your thoughts, doesn't mean that life is meant to or that you can make it comply through sheer discipline and will. This belief is the ego's fantasy and, for many, a source of great suffering.

There will come a time when humans will be evolved enough to manifest through thought alone, but that time is not in the immediate future for most. Spiritual masters and avatars have demonstrated this ability at times, but that doesn't mean just anyone is capable of this. In this case, practice does not make perfect. A certain purity of heart is necessary before the ability to manifest through thought alone is bestowed, and there is great wisdom, Grace, in that gift not being given prematurely.

One reason you believe you have more control over life than you actually do is simply because the ego wants more control. This is called wishful thinking: "I want it to be this way, therefore it is." A belief in control stands in for actual control. This is a coping mechanism on the part of the ego, which helps quell its fears and distrust of life.

The ego wouldn't need this delusion if it perceived life as it actually is: benevolent. It doesn't perceive the goodness, wisdom, love, and joy behind life. The ego is not connected to the truth about life and therefore perpetuates and clings to its own falsehoods. It needs to tell itself lies to protect itself from its own lies. The lie of control is a supposed protection against the ego's fear that it won't survive unless it has control. And yet, the truth is that you do not have much control and you still survive quite well.

In any event, even if more control were possible, that would not be the answer, because the ego, which is divorced from one's innate wisdom, simply doesn't know what choices will lead to a safe, secure, fulfilling, and happy life. It only pretends to know this. The ego has some functionality in terms of protecting people from immediate, impending danger, but being as primitive as it is, that functionality is quite limited and incapable of guiding you in living a good life.

Where you appear to have some control is in small choices. Even if you can't choose whether you will get that job you applied for or who will fall in love with you, you can choose what you will have for breakfast, for instance. However, if we look at even that choice more closely, how much control do you actually have over what you choose for breakfast? What is choosing your breakfast? Isn't it conditioning, including habits, preferences, and what you were taught about breakfast? If your conditioning is choosing your breakfast, are *you* really choosing it? Are *you* controlling even that?

Who is this *you* that wants control and believes it has control? Can you find it? You think you decided to have oatmeal for breakfast, but wouldn't it be more accurate to say that deciding happened? Did it happen *to* anyone? You could say that it happened to your body-mind, since it happened in relation to it, but you are certainly more than your body-mind. So if you are not your body-mind, then who is this *you* that deciding happens to? Is there even such a thing as a *you* that it is happening to, or is it more true to simply say that it is happening?

I'm not suggesting you actually language things this way when speaking with others. That would be awkward. But it is useful to be aware of how inaccurately language depicts reality and how language distances you from the truth about life.

Another way of talking about this is that conditioning gets played out, and either you are aware of that conditioning being played out or you think you are making choices. It's fine if it still feels like you are making choices. You are designed to be that way. You have an illusory you that seems to be making choices and having a life. But in truth, you *are* Life, the Divine, living itself out in the locality of your body-mind.

Sometimes the Divine lets the illusory you and its conditioning have its way, and sometimes the Divine has its way and moves accordingly, if that is required. This happens more often than you probably realize. And so there is a perpetual dance, a back and forth, going on in your life between "your" free will, or your conditioning, and the will of the Divine.

This conditioning can get played out in many different ways: You might have oatmeal today and yogurt tomorrow. So that adds to the illusion of free will. Within the conditioning are many possible choices, and those are the cards you have to play. In any situation, everyone has many possible cards to play, many possible choices they might make, all of which are likely to fall within their conditioning.

So life is by no means predetermined. That would only be the case if everyone had only one possible choice. Life is much more interesting than that! And yet, control and choice are illusions, since conditioning is just playing out. You seem to be choosing, but it is more like certain probabilities are being played out that are connected to your body-mind and its conditioning.

Something very interesting happens when you begin to wake up out of this conditioning. You discover the deeper truth about life: There is, and always has been, another force unfolding and determining your life besides the imaginary you and its conditioning. This force that is living you also entails many possibilities and is highly unpredictable.

Once the existence of this force is realized, you can choose to align more with it instead of letting your conditioning run the show. What is this *you* that can choose this? Now, that is truly mysterious. It is the Divine in you waking up to itself!

There is a mysterious force, a will, that is taking everyone's life in a particular direction. There is a flow, a direction to everyone's life, and within that flow are many possibilities. Out of those possibilities, or probabilities, a particular experience manifests. And yet, amidst this unpredictability and seeming randomness, the flow does have a direction, and something is determining that direction. That something has often been called Thy will, which of course refers to God, the life force, or the intelligence behind all life. This brings us to another truth about life: *The intelligence behind life has a design.*

Allow me to explain how a design naturally results from intelligence. A mark of intelligence is creativity. This is one of the things that sets humans apart from the animal kingdom, which operates largely from instinct. Humans have not only instinct but free will to use their intelligence in various ways. One of those ways is to create.

Design is inherent in creation, whether that design was intentional or not. Even without a particular intention or design initially, a design develops; something is created. The artist or musician, for example, makes some initial choices, one thing leads to another, and something is created that appears to have been designed. Even the most chaotic painting has its own unique design.

Given this, is it so surprising that this thing called life, this universe, also has a design? If you believe there is an intelligence behind life, then it stands to reason that life also has a design or is at the very least being designed as it goes along.

If life has a design (and it does), then that raises many questions: Who or what is designing it, to what purpose, what is each creation's part in it, and how is that design revealed and carried out? That is what the next chapter is about.

CHAPTER 2

The Designer and the Design

The Designer is an unimaginable intelligence. The Designer is not knowable, even by those of us in higher dimensions. It is our understanding, however, that the Designer, the Oneness, always was and always will be, although there was a beginning to creation itself. So at one point, a choice was made to create something from the Oneness.

Creation was an experiment of sorts: What will happen if...? And thus began an evolution of creation and, as a result, an evolution of the Designer. We can only assume that there is no end to creation or to its evolution, although we could also assume that the Designer could bring it all to some kind of completion and return to existing simply as Oneness, Formlessness, without expression.

We, in higher dimensions, can only make assumptions about the Designer and creation based on what we have experienced of the Designer and of creations such as ourselves and others we have encountered. We assume that creation has a purpose, because it seems to serve one. Since creation results in growth and change—evolution—we have to assume that evolution and the results of that are creation's purpose, or at least that that is purpose enough for creation to continue, or it would not.

Other results of creation and its evolution are further creation, enjoyment, surprise, experience, understanding, learning, exploration, discovery, stimulation of curiosity, and problem solving. So these may be purposes of creation as well, although we can't be sure which purposes are most important to the Designer.

Creation may have been created with a certain purpose in mind, and then many other rewards were discovered and became purposes as well. As with everything in life, there are no simple causes and effects. The purpose of creation *is* the effect, whether that was the intention of creation or not.

Among sentient beings, as we know them, are certain common traits. Based on these, we presume to know something about the Designer. Intelligence is the most obvious trait of sentient life. And how do we define intelligence? The ability to think, to problem-solve, to come to conclusions, to plan, to design, to imagine?

These are all capacities of intelligence, but there is something else that is undefinable, mysterious: What is it that *wants* to do these things? Intelligence without will wouldn't bother to think, to solve a problem, to create, to imagine. Will is integral to intelligence. Without it, intelligence would be useless.

Will is very mysterious. What is it? Where does it come from? Who put it there? What is its purpose? If something exists, it must have a purpose. Did the Designer develop intelligence and will, or were they inherent in the Oneness? We will never know the answers to these questions, and we don't need to. More to the point is that intelligence and will are important features of sentient life. You have been given intelligence and will, and presumably the Designer also has these traits, or they could not be made manifest within you.

Other traits that can be assumed to belong to the Designer because they also are universally present in sentient life are love, curiosity, playfulness, and a drive to learn and create. Without these traits, sentient life could never have flourished, evolved, and come into its own as creators.

Granted, these are a lot of assumptions! But we have nothing else to go on beyond such reasoning and our immediate experience of life and of the Oneness, to the extent that we are able to experience the Oneness.

To some, this may sound odd, that I, whom you have known and honored as Jesus the Christ, is not all-knowing, even as I rest in another dimension. But, relatively speaking, I am only slightly more advanced than you. I am able to communicate and relate to you as I do because I have had many human lifetimes on earth. Without those, my role in regard to earth would be limited, for "It takes one to know one," as they say.

Some might also be disturbed by me discussing things of a metaphysical nature, when you don't perceive me as a teacher of metaphysics. But Jesus of Nazareth was only one of my many, many incarnations, indisputably the most recognized and celebrated one.

I, like you, am much more than a particular incarnation and have continued to evolve beyond the enlightened state of that lifetime. Enlightenment marks the end of your lifetimes on earth, unless one chooses to return to earth to serve. Once enlightenment is reached, spiritual evolution continues in other, nonphysical dimensions.

So I am speaking to you as the one you have known as Jesus the Christ; and yet, that is no longer who I am. I am presenting myself as this because it serves a purpose in connecting with you, and it is a way, from this level, that I can continue to teach the universal wisdom I taught then. I appreciate your open-mindedness on this matter, as not everyone is willing to accept the existence of other dimensions. If you can continue to keep an open mind, I will say more about the design.

The design obviously has intelligence behind it—because it works! If you designed something and it works, it is because you had an idea and you tried a number of things until you got it to work. How do we know it works? Because it is predictable. It is governed by laws that are predictable. If you design a watch, for instance, you design it to work predictably, or it would be useless. The laws behind life in your dimension, what you understand as physics, are proof of a design, the intention to design something that works. This intention reflects both intelligence and a will to create, something you have very much in common with the Designer.

Predictability makes creation work, but unpredictability makes it interesting! Creation has been designed to not only work, but also be interesting. Interesting to whom? This points to intelligence as well. Just as you find change, challenge, and interactivity interesting, we can infer from the design that the Designer also enjoys change, challenge, and interactivity. Without unpredictability, the design wouldn't be fun, interesting, or spark growth. Unpredictability allows for endless curiosity, discovery, and evolution.

We saw how predictability was built into the design. How is unpredictability built into the design? Two words: free will. Give some of the creations free will. That makes life interesting and growthful. Free will also turns creatures into creators. However, if all creatures had free will, you would be in trouble!

Some creations are designed to support those who are designed to be creators. Those intended to be creators have free will and those not intended to be creators do not. Good plan, wouldn't you say?

If you were the Designer, how might you make this design even more interesting, fun, challenging, and growthful? Why, you would join in creation rather than stand apart from it! You would *become* the creators you designed instead of just observe them. And why stop there? You would also become every other aspect of creation. You could experience, not just observe, being a bird, a tree, a microbe, a rock, water, an elephant—every aspect of life. What fun! But as creators also, you could manipulate and affect all of life as well. You could experience being everything you created and also have a means of affecting it from inside creation, not only outside of creation.

You are now developing a similar capacity through virtual reality technology. Through that technology, you can experience realities you could never before experience and make choices within those realities that shape those experiences. Such involvement and interactivity is far more interesting than just watching a movie.

Through virtual reality technology, you are expanding and exploring your capacity as creators, and that is only the merest beginning. When you reach our dimension, you will be able to create anything you wish without any technology whatsoever! By then, you will be incapable of creating anything that destroys life before its time.

And now for the most important component of this design: love. What does love bring to the design? Love is the drive behind creation and the glue that holds it all together. The will behind creation is actually love. Isn't that why you create? Isn't the act of creation an expression of love? Without love, you wouldn't act, you wouldn't create, and neither would the Designer, we assume. Love is the driving and shaping force behind all creation. Thy will is carried out by love. Thy will is love made manifest.

I have sometimes also called this force that is love, Grace. I have called Grace the hand of God because Grace is the aspect of God that acts in the world to fulfill Thy will and carry out the divine design. Grace is the mysterious and unseen movement of God upon creation. Grace's movement is motivated by love and indistinct from love. You could no more separate love from Grace than take the wetness out of water. Love is the overarching quality behind Grace because it is the overarching quality of what we have been calling God.

That God is love has become a rather trite saying. Words so often over simplify the mysterious. How can they not? Words and the mind that creates them were not designed to explain the Mystery. Anything that is said about the Mystery is bound to be inadequate, and we will have to accept that. And yet, the Mystery deserves an attempt at understanding and investigating it.

For our purposes, it is not important or necessary to try to describe God in words. It is only important that you understand one thing: God is benevolent. The Designer is benevolent, and the proof is that love is what propels the Designer and shapes creation, and this is what I intend to prove to you.

It is important for you to know this, because deeply realizing this can change your life by shifting your state of consciousness. Knowing that you are loved, cared for, and supported by the Designer and that you have an important place and purpose in the design has the potential for transforming your outlook on life. Knowing this can shift you from the ego's perspective of separation, fear, lack, and conflict with life to one that allows you to be at peace with life and to fall in love with it and be happy.

This falling in love with life is a return to your divine nature, which is in love with life. As God, you are completely head-over-heels in love with life! I know this because it is my experience and that of those in other dimensions beyond your own. It can be your experience as well—and it is meant to be. The experiences you have had and are having have been orchestrated to bring you to a realization of your true nature and to the love and happiness at your core.

In describing the Designer and the design, my purpose is to help you realize your true nature. This is not an exercise in trying to put the impossible into words, but trying to open your minds to the possibility that you are the very force of life that has set your life in motion.

You are the created and the Creator, the Form and the Formless. You are All That Is expressing itself in your little corner of the universe, which gives you a unique standpoint and role in all of creation. You are here to serve creation from this unique standpoint. That is your essential purpose. This purpose is known and carried out through love.

You also have a more specific purpose, which is revealed in each moment. This moment-to-moment purpose is also known and carried out through love. You know what this purpose is because it is whatever you are loving in any moment. What are you loving now? Whatever your attention is being given to is what you are loving, and no matter what that is, there is a purpose in that:

❖ *If you are loving your negative thoughts by giving your attention to them, then the purpose in that moment is to experience the result of doing that and learn from that.*

❖ *If you are loving a tree by giving your attention to that tree, then the purpose in that moment is to experience the tree-ness of that tree.*

❖ *If you are loving your anger by feeding it with more thoughts, then the purpose in that moment is to experience the result of doing that and learn from that.*

❖ *If you are giving your attention to feeling grateful, then the purpose in that moment is to have the experience of gratitude and discover the result of that.*

❖ *If your love is flowing to another person, then the purpose in that moment is to experience what it is like to give your love to that person.*

Giving your attention, your love, to something brings you a certain experience and thereby teaches you something. You may not be aware of what you are learning or that you are learning by simply experiencing something, but you are always learning at least one thing: the result of giving your attention to whatever you are giving your attention to. If the result is pleasant, you learn one thing; if the result is unpleasant, you learn something else. Whatever the result, you are learning something, and probably a number of things.

Experience equals learning. It is impossible not to learn from your experiences. Giving your attention, your love, to whatever you are giving it to is how the Divine, through you, experiences life and evolves. This is going on in every moment, and it is the most basic purpose of each of your lives.

The awareness you have been given as a conscious, sentient being—this ability to attend to life—is the only way the

Creator can experience the life you are living. The Creator is aware through the sensory apparatus of your body-mind. But the experience is even more intimate than that: This awareness *is* the Creator looking through your eyes.

The Creator is looking through the eyes of the human being it is pretending to be, which it has created for that purpose. Sometimes the egoic programming is directing that attention and sometimes the Creator is. The seeming separate person, made possible through programming, is learning by giving his or her attention (love) to one thing after another and noting the result. And the Creator is learning both vicariously through the character and through its own direct experience of life. Love, the willingness to engage with and attend to the many wondrous aspects of this world, drives the learning and evolution of both the person and the Creator.

Love is also the lesson that is learned, although along the way many other things are learned as well, including things the Creator didn't know would be learned. Creation is an experiment for the Creator, an unknown adventure without an end, but one with the intention to experience, grow, learn, create, and have fun. What will be learned? Who knows? Knowing that would only take the fun out of it.

Love is the glue, the common thread, and what drives the adventure, informs it, and keeps the Creator from getting lost completely in creation. Love is also the destination. The adventure's ultimate purpose is to rediscover love after having lost it to the egoic state of consciousness.

This purpose gives the adventure a direction. Love, as Grace, is the secret ingredient embedded in creation that guides people and leads them Home. Grace drops the "breadcrumbs" that show you the way.

The illusion of being a separate self is a very powerful one, as you well know, since you are living it. And it is one fully of confusion and suffering. However, if the Illusion were completely pleasurable and made sense, there would be no drive to question it or find a way out. The Illusion is meant to be unpleasant for a reason: The players in this game called life are meant to find their way out of illusion to the Truth.

Suffering motivates you to find the Truth, and love shows you the way out. The players are given the challenge of having an ego that doesn't know or trust love, and they must discover that the key to life is love. The suffering in being divorced from one's true nature, from love, drives them to the ultimate discovery—that love is all that matters. Love is the reason and reward for existing. Once you have deeply realized this, you have won the game. Built into the game of life is this endgame.

You cannot play the game without it ending this way. That is really good news. As a result, there are no wrong choices, since every choice eventually leads to the same outcome: love. But how you play this game is up to you. Everyone plays it differently, according to their particular programming, what they have learned along the way, and how in touch they are with their divine self.

As you learn and grow, you begin to awaken from your programming, from the Illusion, and your divine self takes on a greater role in your life. You are no longer the victim of your programming nor are you defined by it. As you come to know your true self, you more consciously, or intentionally, use whatever programming still works for you, while overwriting and replacing any that doesn't serve you with new ways of being.

You have been given the freedom to become free. It is the loving hand of Grace that guides you to that freedom. What good would free will be if it didn't take you to freedom from the pain and suffering of the Illusion? To be free to choose within the Illusion is a limited freedom indeed.

You are given the freedom to choose so that you can not only have experiences within the Illusion, but also become free of it. Your freedom to choose enables you to eventually discover the Truth, the love at your core. God is benevolent indeed! What chooses to become free from the Illusion is the divine self awakening in you when it is time for that to happen.

The fact that Grace guides you on your journey within the Illusion is also a sign of great benevolence and love. You have been given programming and free will to shape this journey. But, importantly, you have also been given a plan—a divinely inspired destiny—and Grace, the shaping hand of God, to deliver that plan and help you fulfill it.

This plan was developed by your soul with the help of nonphysical beings before you entered this lifetime. It includes lessons, talents, gifts, opportunities, and certain destined events and meetings with people with whom you have soul agreements. Your soul's plan is a blueprint, but without the details spelled out.

The details are filled in by your choices and also determined by the circumstances in which you find yourself. For instance, if your choices led to you living in a particular city, then that location provides the setting, environment, and people your soul must work with to bring about your plan. These circumstances were not known by your soul prior to you being born.

Although certain things are predetermined before birth, such as your parents and your place of birth, how your life will play out and where is largely unknown to the soul. The soul has to play it by ear and arrange the opportunities, lessons, meetings, and other circumstances to fulfill your plan as best it can within the existing conditions. As a result, your soul must be in touch with you closely throughout your life, which it does through the Heart: the intuition.

Grace's primary means for shaping and steering people's lives is through the intuition, which works surprisingly well. People respond quite easily to their own intuition if their mind doesn't interfere and also to intuitive nudges to do and say things for others. People quite naturally deliver messages to others, especially if the one delivering the message has no self-interest in the matter or opinions about the person the message is for. As a result, Grace often works through disinterested or unrelated parties: Someone unknown to you tells you something or does something for you that changes your direction or even your life. This happens all the time.

Fortunately, there are many ways your plan can be fulfilled. How that is done specifically is generally left up to free will, but Grace intervenes to bring certain opportunities and limit others. Grace is like a hand that puts certain people, opportunities, and information in front of you, which you can say yes or no to. If you say no to an important opportunity, Grace may provide another suitable one or arrange circumstances that help you see the benefit of saying yes to the original opportunity. Grace can be very convincing! It can make certain opportunities difficult to dismiss and certain directions difficult to pursue.

This hand of Grace, which arranges and prohibits certain events in your life and in the world, is more of a real force than you may realize. Although I would never suggest that people are puppets in relation to this force, there are strings on you that get pulled from time to time, although you can always go against them.

These strings are pulled by nonphysical forces. Their job is to manage the comings and goings in life in a way that keeps them moving in a particular direction according to everyone's soul's plan, the larger plan for earth, and the even larger plan for the Whole.

There is both free will and something controlling the unfolding of your life and life in general. You fit into a much larger picture, a much larger unfolding: a design. Your life has a design within the greater design. However, exactly how these designs unfold is in no one's control because everyone's free will is determining this.

The number of players affecting how things unfold is beyond imagination, as everyone on earth is a player as well as nonphysical players in other dimensions. Just think: Everyone on earth is a player in your destiny, and you are a player in theirs! It would be even more accurate to say that everyone who has ever lived on earth has been a player in your destiny, but even that doesn't begin to cover it.

The larger game plan involves players you have never imagined existed, as the Whole within which this unfolding is taking place involves not only Earth, but also other planets within your universe and an infinite number of other universes and dimensions related to those. Fortunately, you don't need to be aware of or understand anything other than your immediate corner of the universe. That is what you are here for—your particular life and experience.

This life of yours is being guided by extremely wise and benevolent forces. You are in good hands. The hand of Grace is eminently intelligent and wise, far beyond your imagination. And you are honored and loved so deeply, also beyond your imagination. I cannot emphasize this enough. If you only knew how treasured each and every one of you are!

If you don't know how loved you are, it is more difficult for the hand of Grace to operate in your life. If you are very lost in the Illusion, in believing you are not lovable, not loved, or alone or abandoned by an uncaring world or universe, you won't be able to take advantage of all the opportunities and abundance available to you. You won't recognize or be willing to receive what is being offered.

When you are lost in your fears and feelings of not being good enough, the reality you experience is a scary and limited one. You filter out anything that doesn't fit your negative perspective. You filter out the positive in life and look right past or misinterpret the helping hands, kind words, encouragement, gentle nudges, and out-and-out gifts that life—Grace—is offering you. You fail to see the goodness in life.

When you are lost in the Illusion, nonphysical forces allow you to have that experience until you have had enough and are done choosing it, however unconscious that choice might be. Because they honor your free will, nonphysical forces will not interfere in your choices.

When you are lost, these forces still try to help you see the truth about your situation, but they can only do so much to help you as long as you aren't asking or looking to them or to others for help. Without their help or the help of others, the primary means of awakening you from the Illusion is the suffering caused by the Illusion itself.

Here are some examples of how Grace operates in people's lives:

❖ *Your father's friend helps you get your first job.*

❖ *You don't have the money to go to college, but you're able to get a loan. (Yes, Grace works through governments and banks too.)*

❖ *Your aunt gives you enough money to pay your rent for a few months while you look for a job.*

❖ *Your friend needs a roommate at exactly the same time you need a place to live.*

❖ *Someone offers you another job just when you were thinking of leaving your old one.*

❖ *You always wanted to go to Europe, and then a friend invites you to go along with her family.*

❖ *You read about something and realize you'd like to learn more about it.*

❖ *You have a health problem, and you run into someone with the same problem who has found some answers.*

❖ *You don't know how to do something, so you search YouTube and find a video that shows you. (The universe provides! But sometimes you have to find your way to those resources, in which case you will be led intuitively.)*

❖ *A friend gives you her ticket to a concert because she got sick, and you meet the love of your life there.*

These kinds of things happen in everyone's life—often. How many have happened to you that you simply ignored or said no to or didn't take full advantage of? Life is made of such opportunities They come out of the flow regularly. This is life happening to you and for you.

Life is so benevolent that if you miss an opportunity that is significant to your plan's unfolding, you'll be presented with it again or with some other opportunity. Life says: "Okay. How about this then?" Grace allows you to make whatever choices you make, all the while presenting you with many possibilities to choose from. These possibilities and all the pointers to them from other people are the hand of Grace in your life. They are not random, meaningless occurrences but a meaningful part of a greater design.

That is not to say that everything that happens to you is part of your design. People have free will, and when they are choosing from their egos, the opportunities or suggestions they offer will not necessarily be aligned with your plan. Egos have their own agendas, which are only sometimes helpful to your plan. Out of the flow come both opportunities from Grace and opportunities from egos, whose free will choices affect you and may influence you in directions not in keeping with your soul's plan.

The most problematic ego of all is your own. Your egoic programming has its own ideas about how life should unfold, how your life should look, what it wants and needs, and how to go about getting that. Your free will in the hands of your ego instead of surrendered to Grace is the greatest obstacle to taking advantage of what Grace has to offer.

Moment to moment, Grace presents its opportunities and delivers its "instructions" for how to live your life. If you aren't aware that Grace is doing this, you may miss those opportunities or instructions, which manifest as intuitions and subtle inner drives, urges, impulses, and inspiration. If you are lost in your thoughts, which are your ego's thoughts, about what you should do and how your life should look, you'll miss how your life is actually unfolding—right in front of you. Your life is being given to you and being shown to you moment to moment.

Your life is happening to you on its own. But you are free to choose to try to create another life, one the ego imagines or fantasizes about, or one that someone else is living or seems to be living, like on TV. You can live inside your head, in your ideas about yourself and your life, or try to, or you can live the life you are being given.

You are given a particular life to live. You have quite a lot of choice within the life you are given. You even have the choice to reject the life you are given. But you aren't given the choice to live a completely different life, someone else's life.

People suffer so greatly over not being able to have someone else's life! They believe they can make their life be anything they want. When they discover they can't, they are disappointed and angry with life and with themselves. But that suffering is unnecessary. Everyone can find happiness. When you live the life that is meant for you, you will be content. This contentment is how Grace rewards you for saying yes to it and finding your place in the universe.

CHAPTER 3

Seeing the Good

The Designer and the design are good. Life is good! This is another truth about life. Let us contemplate the nature of goodness for a moment. What is it? You know what it is because goodness is basic to your experience as a human being. Even if you don't generally experience it within yourself, you can still experience it in others because it is also within you. And if you look for it, you will also be able to find it in yourself.

Even the most hardened person can be melted at the sight of a puppy. Why? Because that puppy (and all of creation) reflects your own inherent goodness back to you. The innocence of a puppy, a baby, or even a tree is that goodness. When you are stripped bare of all of your ideas about yourself and everything else, you are that innocence too. It is what you *are*. You are that goodness.

You cannot *not* know what goodness is. It is love, of course. But for the purposes of this chapter, we are going to call this love *goodness* so that you can know the goodness within yourself more fully.

Words can be useful that way. They are pointers. The word *goodness* is something unreal that points to something real. It may seem funny to say that goodness is real, when reality is generally thought of as something solid, tangible, or at least something that can be sensed. Goodness doesn't appear real to the mind and senses in the way a chair does, and yet goodness is more real than anything that can be sensed. Still, you do sense goodness. But you sense it with something subtler than eyes or ears, something you may not even be aware of because you are swimming in it: Awareness.

You are able to sense and experience goodness and everything else because you are aware, conscious. Consciousness had to exist first before you could be aware of reality. This Awareness *is* reality. This aware consciousness is immersed in, inseparable from, and expressing through reality. Everything is steeped in consciousness. Everything *is* consciousness.

Because this Awareness *is* reality, it can know itself. It knows itself well—intimately, of course. You know it, your true nature, intimately too. It is just that your true nature is so close that it can't be experienced with your five senses. It is what is using your senses, which is why your senses can't sense it. Although you can't see what you are, that doesn't make it less real but more real. The realest thing around is *you,* the aware consciousness that is looking out of your eyes and using your senses to experience physical reality.

Awareness, through your body-mind, senses not only physical reality, but also itself as reality and within reality. It senses itself as the goodness, love, peace, beauty, and perfection that exist as creation. It senses what is beyond and behind the physical representation of reality. It senses the ground from which physical reality springs: the Formless. Awareness knows the Formless because it is the Formless. It knows itself.

You know yourself, but you don't always know that you do. Sometimes you are in touch with your true nature, and sometimes you are not. You get lost in the play of light on physical reality. You believe physical reality. But physical reality couldn't exist without the Formless.

You get lost in the experience of physical reality and forget the Formless. But most of all, you get lost in your ideas about physical reality, including your ideas about yourself. Your mental reality becomes your reality, your experience. That mental reality is removed not only from form but from the Formless.

The way back to the Formless, then, is from the mental reality to the physical reality, and then to the Formless behind physical reality. It is very difficult to move from the mental reality straight to the Formless. And when you are caught in the mental realm, it doesn't occur to you to do this, unless you encounter spiritual teachings that suggest this.

Sensory experience—direct sensing of physical reality without interference from the mind—is the doorway to the Formless and to the experience of your true nature. You must go through physical reality to get to the Truth. Form will take you to the Formless, but the mind won't. Thinking won't because it wasn't designed to.

The mind takes you into an imaginary reality, away from the Truth. That is not a problem if you aren't seeking the Formless. It's fun to play in the mental realm and explore imaginary possibilities, which is why you so enjoy movies and novels. But we are exploring the Truth here, and for that, the mind is not useful. It can't take you to the Truth; it can only point to the Truth, as I am doing now. To experience the Truth, you have to leave the mind behind.

To explore the Truth, you need another kind of instrument, one as subtle as the Truth. This makes sense: You need physical instruments to explore physical reality, so you need something of the nature of the Formless to explore the Formless. Fortunately, you have been given such an instrument: the Heart.

You are given everything you need to be happy and fulfilled, and the Heart is the most important gift of all. Even if you were not given hands or eyes or ears, you have the most essential sensing device of all: the spiritual Heart. It is always available to you, and no one can take it from you. But like any other tool, you have to choose to use it. However, your default tool, the one you naturally go to for everything, is the mind.

The Heart is the sensing device of the soul, the connector to the soul, and the delivery station of the soul's information. The soul carries and administers your life plan with the help of nonphysical beings, who orchestrate the activities on earth and elsewhere. The information you need to lead the life you are meant to live, from your soul's perspective, is given to you through the Heart.

As mysterious as the Heart is, the Heart is actually very familiar to you and more real than your body. It is more real in that it is eternal, everlasting. It is who you are. It is the aspect of God within you, the life force that is living you.

The word *Heart* makes the Heart seem like a thing, as if it has a location and size, as if it could fit inside your body. Any word we give it makes it small, turns it into a thing. That is the limitation of language. But this Heart is not just your Heart; it does not belong to the character you are playing. It is the Heart of All and in all. The very same Heart is in everything. And yet, it contains the specific information you need to live this lifetime as the character you have chosen to be.

The Heart not only conveys information about your soul's plan to you, but also guides you through your life moment to moment. Imagine that! And all along, you thought the voice in your head was your trusty guide. That's not your fault, of course. You and everyone else were programmed to rely on the voice in your head. How convenient to have someone in your head telling you what to do, when to do it, and who you are! Too bad that voice is so unreliable.

Unlike that voice, the Heart is reliable and doesn't tell you what to do and when to do it or even who you are. The Heart allows and accepts whatever you choose to do and whoever you choose to be, while patiently delivering its suggestions. It doesn't push you, hurry you, or scare you. The Heart rarely uses words, although it might use a few if need be to save your life or help you avoid an accident. Otherwise, the Heart communicates in other ways, mostly intuitively. The hints it drops are experienced as an insight or "aha!" It also nudges you gently through subtle urges, impulses, and drives.

And unlike the voice in your head, the Heart doesn't communicate nonstop but only when needed. Just as your car's GPS doesn't constantly speak to you when you are on course, neither does your Heart. It only speaks to you when you need to make a change or if you go off course. Then the Heart comes online, not as thoughts, but as an intuitive sense of being off and a sense of needing to reorient. Then the Heart continues to give you direction through your intuition until you are solidly on course again.

The Heart also lets you know moment to moment where your consciousness is: whether it is identified with your thoughts and the imaginary you or expanded, free, and in touch with your divine self, or somewhere in between. This information is delivered through a sense of relaxation and peace when you are aligned with your divine self, or tension and contraction when you are not. Tension and contraction are signs that you are caught in the Illusion, believing some thought. The degree of contraction is the degree to which you are caught in that mistaken belief.

When you are feeling contracted, your intuition may kick in to try to help you shift out of believing or doing whatever is causing the contraction. Your Heart is always working to make you happier! For instance, when you are pushing yourself too hard, you might suddenly see that. Then in that moment of clarity, a choice can be made to continue pushing yourself or to stop.

That sudden insight or ability to see the situation from a higher, truer perspective is your divine self inserting itself, its truth, into the situation. Then it is up to you to make a change or not. If you don't, your divine self may continue to insert itself in similar ways, or maybe someone in your environment will suggest you stop and take a break, as others are often messengers for what one needs to hear.

These intuitive insights are little glimpses of the truth, brief apertures that give you a snapshot of another possibility, another way of being that is not determined by your ego. If you are aware enough and committed to being free of the tyranny and distortions of the egoic illusion, you may be able to summon your will in that moment and change course. The more you use your will to shift your consciousness this way, the easier this becomes, and the Illusion will begin to lose its grip on you.

There is goodness, Grace, in the fact that you are given a way out of the Illusion. There is also goodness in the fact that you have been given a body that registers the truth. Through contraction, tension, stress, and negative emotions, your body lets you know when you are lost in the Illusion. And when you are in touch with the truth about life, your body tells you that as well through relaxation, peace, contentment, and happiness.

In this way, Grace trains you to go Home and shows you when you are Home. But first you have to realize that there is such a place as Home. Not everyone is aware of a possibility other than suffering, and even if they are, they might not feel deserving of love and peace. These are the two biggest blocks to seeing and receiving Grace's bounty.

Grace — the goodness and helping hand underlying life — is always there:

❖ *Inspiring you to act and create,*

❖ *Bringing you the information you need,*

❖ *Bringing you the relationships you need,*

❖ *Bringing you those who are here to serve you and those you are here to serve,*

❖ *Bringing you the jobs you need,*

❖ *Bringing you whatever help you need,*

❖ *Bringing you understanding and insights,*

❖ *Bringing you the circumstances in which you can best evolve,*

❖ *Bringing you the strength to persist when that is needed,*

❖ *Encouraging you to develop your talents,*

❖ *Encouraging you to grow and learn,*

❖ *Encouraging you (giving you courage) to stay aligned with the Truth,*

❖ *Nudging you when you need nudging,*

❖   *Showing you the way when you've gotten lost,*

❖   *Helping you carry on when you're hurting,*

❖   *Helping you get up when you have fallen,*

❖   *Helping you see the positive,*

❖   *Allowing you to make mistakes, while bringing you the means for learning from them,*

❖   *Loving you,*

❖   *Healing you,*

❖   *Bringing you joy and love,*

❖   *Guiding you, and*

❖   *Watching over and protecting you.*

You are never alone. If only you knew this! If only you knew the bounty that is offered you in every moment, you could take advantage of those gifts. Those who do know this are able to shine and fulfill their greatest potential.

The ego keeps you trapped in a world where you believe you are alone, without sufficient resources, unguided except for the mind, and uncherished (just one of the crowd). You feel more like a street urchin than what you actually are: the child of an incomprehensibly powerful, good, and generous father.

You have everything you need to be happy and flourish. But because most of you don't know that, it is as if you don't have those things. It's like having a bank account you aren't aware of or a wealthy, loving family you've never met. If you don't know you have these, it is the same as not having them. But if you know they belong to you, you will claim them.

If you look for Grace in your life, you will find it. But you have to look for it. Looking opens the door to realizing that

Grace has always been there. Unless you open that door, you will keep living on the other side of that door. Living in the egoic state of consciousness is like living in a small room with no windows. You have no idea what is outside that room, but that room is familiar and it seems safe, while anything else seems strange and scary.

The ego is afraid to have you look outside that room. It tries to talk you into staying inside: "Isn't this good enough? It's dangerous out there. You'd be foolish to go exploring. You'll get lost. Everyone will think you're crazy. You'll be alone." Whether these are the mind's actual messages or not, a deep-seated fear and disbelief in one's own power keep people doing what they have always done and listening to what they have always listened to: their mind and other people's minds. What else is there? Many people don't know there is something else that is meant to guide them, something that will make them supremely happy.

To hear the still, small voice of your intuition, of the Heart, you have to listen very carefully. You have to be very dedicated to hearing and following it because it will not insist that you listen to it. Unlike the voice in your head, the Heart will not give you reasons to listen to it or try to convince you of its point of view

The Heart speaks without words, gently, patiently, and kindly. And if you say no to it, it will honor that choice. The Heart will wait until you are ready to turn to it and seek out its answers for yourself. Then you will begin to hear the Heart more clearly and realize the help that is there for you.

Then there is one more step: You have to choose to follow that voice, which is where many get tripped up. They hear the Heart's voice, but they let the voice in their head talk them out of following their Heart. This tendency is not easily overcome.

The programming that compels you to listen to and believe the voice in your head is not disabled overnight. It is the most insistent programming of all.

If you weren't programmed to believe your thoughts (despite how untrue most of them are), the Illusion could not be sustained. Believing your egoic thoughts is what upholds the Illusion. The only way to break out of the Illusion is to stop believing those thoughts, or do the best you can little by little. Every mistaken belief that is seen through weakens the Illusion, making it easier to see the Illusion for what it is. Then what is left is the Heart's guidance.

You have always been following the Heart's guidance to some extent. As silent and unimposing as the Heart is, it is nevertheless the only thing living your life. The Heart allows you to believe your thoughts and pretend that you are what they say you are until you are ready to see the truth about them. Meanwhile, the Heart delivers guidance in the ways it can: through inspiration, impulses, motivation, urges, drives, excitement, attraction, and joy. In every moment, the Heart steers you using these subtle communications.

You already know these communications well. You can't help but follow the Heart's nudges, drives, joy, and inspiration at least some of the time, since following your Heart feels good. So when you shift from following the mind to following the Heart, you will just be doing more of what you already know how to do, and you will do it more consciously, more intentionally.

Life leads you with joy, excitement, and a sense of rightness. The flow takes you where you are meant to go by rewarding you with these good feelings. Of course, when you are not going with the flow, that doesn't feel good, but then that alsc is the right experience. Going in the wrong direction is not meant to feel good. Still, you can choose it if you want.

So this is how life works: It steers you with feeling good and feeling bad. Feeling bad, therefore, is not proof that life isn't good or that you aren't good enough. Feeling bad is simply pointing to another way of being or in another direction that *is* good, that is more rewarding. By showing you what makes you feel bad, life is helping you discover what makes you feel good.

Since you are programmed to seek happiness, you might conclude that the purpose of life is to find happiness. However, that would be much too small a goal. The Designer has a much loftier plan than feeling good. Happiness is offered simply as an incentive for a higher goal. That goal is to fulfill your life purpose. The Designer designed you for a specific purpose, and when you are serving that purpose, you feel happy.

This is how the Designer makes the world go around. A happy world is one in which everyone knows their place, their role in the Whole, and is happily playing their part. Your world isn't exactly there yet, but it will be someday. The outmoded and unnecessary voice in people's heads will eventually disappear for everyone, then little will be in the way of fulfilling one's purpose.

Meanwhile, the task is to find happiness now despite the egoic mind. One way to become happier is to look for the goodness in life, which is something the egoic mind can't help you with. For this, you need other eyes, ones that can see beyond the Illusion to what is really here. These eyes have to be developed, cultivated, by using them. You have to learn to perceive through eyes that see clearly and truly: the eyes of your divine self. This is the Heart.

The fact that you have a Heart is proof of the goodness behind life, and it is the Heart that is able to perceive this goodness. The more you practice seeing goodness in your life, the more this capacity of the Heart is developed. This capacity develops until the Truth becomes crystal clear. When that happens, the result is gratitude for all of life.

Gratitude is both a sign that you are seeing through the eyes of the divine self and a means for shifting your gaze from the ego's perspective to the divine self's. Gratitude is both a tool that takes you Home and a means of knowing when you have arrived.

Gratitude, like peace and love, is a quality of your true nature. Your divine self is deeply grateful for life in a physical body and for the opportunity that affords to learn, explore, create, grow, and love. These are the general purposes of the Oneness for coming into a body. But it also has a more specific purpose for every individual, which is discovered and fulfilled by following your joy.

Joy is another quality of your true nature. When you follow joy, it takes you Home. And, like gratitude, calling forth joy from within yourself can shift you from the egoic state of consciousness to the peace and love of your true nature.

This might sound like a Catch-22: To experience joy, you have to experience joy. But that's not what I'm saying. Rather, to experience joy, you simply have to be *willing* to experience it, willing to call it forth. That willingness and intention to experience joy takes you to joy. When you open to joy, it arrives. That is how benevolent and supportive life is. Like a magic wand, trusting that joy is available brings it to the forefront. Joy has always been there, hiding in plain sight.

By rewarding you with joy for simply opening to joy, life teaches you to say yes to the Truth. Life also teaches you that when you say yes to the negative, that is what you get: The negative comes to the forefront or stays in the forefront, and that becomes your experience of life. You are powerful! You may not have much control over life, but you have been given a lot of power: the power to determine how you experience life and what you experience in life.

There is so much to experience in life. What you give your attention to among those many possibilities is what you experience. Give it to the egoic mind's negativity, and you get that Give it to joy, peace, love, or gratitude, and you get that. The Divine, the Father, is like the kindest, wisest parent: A wise parent knows not to reward the child for unloving or harmful behavior but for developing in directions that are of benefit to the child.

All of this shaping of behavior on the part of the Divine is not for the Divine's pleasure or whim but for the good of the Whole, which is also the good of the individual. And that is more proof of the goodness behind life: The purpose of life is for the growth, learning, expansion, and creativity of the Whole, which is accomplished through the growth, learning, expansion, and creativity of the individual. What is good for the Whole is also good for the individual and vice versa. The Designer has learned a thing or two about design, and the Designer knows what works! In creation, love works, goodness works.

Without love, it would be impossible for creation to function, just as societies function only to the degree that they are founded on love. This is because the Whole and the parts are not actually separate, so it would be impossible for them to be at odds. Would your arms be at odds with your body? Why would they? Would it even be possible? Love is the natural cooperation of the Oneness with the created parts of itself. Love makes your bodies and the world work, to the extent that love is not hindered by ego-driven impulses and destructive emotions.

There is a knowing of the Truth in the cells of your very own being. The cells cooperate perfectly with each other in their natural state, and so would people if it were not for the egoic mind. It sets individuals at odds with themselves, each other, and the Whole. The egoic mind makes it difficult for individuals to find their place in the Whole.

That is the challenge: How do you wake up from the Illusion created by the egoic mind? You are finding that out right now. What a great discovery! Can you feel the Divine in you enjoying this discovery? Can you feel the Divine's excitement in it? Your enjoyment and excitement is the Divine's joy in life.

Joy *is* love. You could say that joy is a quality of love or that love is a quality of joy. They are indistinct in one's experience. When you are experiencing one, you are experiencing the other. When you touch something with love, that is, when you are present enough to something that your love flows to it, you experience joy. You are rewarded for loving with joy. So let's explore love for a moment.

Love is who you are. This means that whenever you are being who you really are without any interference from thinking that you are the imaginary you, you experience love. The only way you cannot experience this love is if you are busy experiencing something else, such as your thoughts. This, of course, is the human predicament. People experience their thoughts about life more than they experience real life.

This is surprising isn't it? Most people experience most moments through a veil of ideas. For instance, you see a chair, but what you really see is "the chair Grandma gave me when I was a little girl." Or you see a person, but what you really see is "that person is old." Or you feel an unusual sensation, and you worry that something is terribly wrong. Or you have an experience, and you think, "That shouldn't have happened."

Such thoughts are instantly followed by a feeling, which makes the Illusion spun by that thought seem even more real and true. In the illusory reality, chairs are not just chairs, people are not just people, sensations are not just sensations, and experiences are not just experiences. The mind turns whatever you are experiencing into a story and feelings. That is the illusory world in which your illusory self lives.

This mind-generated reality is made up of beliefs and stories about yourself, others, your experiences, and life in general. These ideas color and distort reality, making it difficult to be in touch with the love that naturally flows from your being to life moment to moment. The ego's misperceptions and stories block this flow of love. To unblock it, reality needs to be perceived clearly, as it actually is. The love, the goodness, needs to be perceived.

What does goodness look like? You know goodness when you see it by how you feel when you see it. Perceiving goodness puts you in touch with your own goodness. Goodness perceives goodness and is reflected back to you. This can operate like a positive feedback loop: The more you stay with the experience of goodness, the stronger the feeling of goodness inside you becomes. Goodness, of course, feels like love and joy, which are the reward for perceiving goodness.

Seeing goodness is a choice on your part, which can be made in any moment. Consciously or unconsciously, you choose what you give your attention to, what you focus on. You can consciously choose to see goodness, and you can cultivate this choice so that it becomes more automatic.

The more consciously you choose to perceive goodness, the happier you can become. Making the intention to perceive goodness activates the goodness within you, and that feels good! Perceiving goodness feels good! This is one way to make yourself happy.

Just as it is in your power to experience joy, it is in your power to see goodness in something, in anything: in a piece of fruit, a kind act, someone's eyes, a dog, a beautiful sound, even a color. The ability to see goodness is innate in you. All you have to do is be willing to see it. You open yourself up to that possibility, and then the experience of goodness is given to you. It happens. It isn't really something you do but, rather, an experience you allow yourself to receive. You pay attention to something long enough to realize that goodness is there.

For example, when someone is kind to you, you can notice how that kindness opens your Heart, if only for a second. How long your Heart stays open depends on how long you attend to and nurture the feeling of goodness and gratitude produced by that kind act. Every act of love, whether you are receiving love or giving it, is an opportunity to experience the goodness within you.

To experience goodness in an object, the object doesn't have to be beautiful in the usual sense, since everything has its own beauty. Nevertheless, a beautiful sky or flower is often easier to see goodness in than a threatening sky or a wilted flower because of one's associations. However, once you are used to seeing goodness in beautiful things, seeing goodness in more ordinary things becomes easier.

Notice how you feel when you let your gaze take in something of beauty without labeling it or commenting mentally about it. Beauty naturally and easily opens the Heart. Notice how this experience feels energetically in your body. Goodness feels a certain way in the body. This experience is difficult to describe, but fortunately descriptions aren't necessary because you already know this feeling.

So when you experience the goodness in the beauty of nature or in a person or an object, just notice that and linger in that experience. This beauty and its goodness is a gift to you. It is the reward for being human, for having a body and senses. You were given these to be able to sense your own and life's beauty and goodness. God is loving you and everything else through you, through the remarkable instrument that is your body.

Can you also experience the goodness of the body you inhabit and the gift that it is? If you don't bring any ideas to this amazing thing that is your body but just, for instance, experience those fingers as they fly across the keyboard, as if they have a mind of their own—which they do. What goodness it is that you are capable of such a feat as typing—and reading! What a marvel you are that you can do everything you do. What goodness is behind the intelligence that enables you to do these things! Everything you are able to do is a gift, a miracle.

You are the greatest miracle of all, for your intelligence and design is particularly well suited to evolving, more so than animals and plants, whose evolution is slower and more circumscribed. You are capable of becoming creators in ways that other creations cannot. What Grace it is that you have been given such a capability! This allows you to experience fun, joy, excitement, discovery, and curiosity, which other creations will never know. What Grace the life you have been given is!

And this planet: It provides for your every need, and then some. What a gift! What goodness! The rain supplies the water needed by every living thing. The sun warms you, lights your life, and delivers the energy that supports the life that sustains you. The soil furnishes the nutrients needed for all of life.

Everything supports everything else in this most magnificent and intricate ecosystem, which deftly adapts and evolves as needed. What Grace that life is so intelligent that it knows exactly how to grow, how to survive, how to adapt, and how to serve the rest of creation! Life supports life. Everything is here to serve everything else. How loving, how kind, how good!

And then there are the eyes. Can you see goodness in people's eyes? Goodness is there so strongly in some, while in others it is clouded over by thoughts, temporarily lost to the Illusion. The eyes are where the divine self is most visible. The same divine being is looking out of everyone's eyes. What looks is the same in everyone, the same Oneness in different guises.

What do you see in the eyes of those whose eyes are clear? In the Dalai Lama, for instance? Sweetness! Goodness. Love. Delight. That is your true nature. Have I convinced you yet? Look for yourself and see where you can find this goodness. Discover it and nurture it within yourself and others. This small act will change the world.

CHAPTER 4

When Bad Things Happen…

When people hear that goodness and love are behind life, they wonder why bad things happen, even to good people. Life seems unfair at times, and it is certainly difficult. Why is life so difficult? And why does it seem unfair? If God is good, then why is there suffering?

These are deep questions and ones that religions have tried to answer, although often unsatisfactorily. If they had been more successful, there would be less suffering. That is not to say that religions haven't brought some comfort to people; they have, because they all teach some of the Truth. However, some of the Truth is not enough to end suffering, especially when much of what religions teach are distortions of the Truth, thanks to the ego. Rather than ending suffering, much of what is taught by religions upholds the Illusion and is therefore incapable of freeing people from it.

The truth about life is such that it eradicates the mistaken ideas that maintain the Illusion and frees people from suffering. The Illusion is the cause of suffering, and the Truth sets you free from those misperceptions. To be free of suffering, the truth about life must be understood, and even then, understanding is not enough. The truth about life also has to be realized experientially to some extent, not only understood intellectually. Understanding prepares one for a deeper realization of the Truth. But, unlike understanding, realization is not up to you; it is up to Grace. Realization is one of the many things you are not in control of — your soul is.

An absence or diminishment of suffering is an indication of some realization. There are many degrees, or depths, of realization and therefore varying degrees of freedom from suffering. There are people who do not suffer or suffer very little, and this gives hope to others. These individuals are said to be awakened or enlightened. What do they understand that others do not? What have they realized? What are the missing pieces to one's understanding of life that, when filled in, will lead to less suffering?

Suffering is largely a result of not being in touch with what is real and true about life and believing things about life that are not true. This is a description of the Illusion: It keeps you out of touch with what is real and true and keeps you believing what is not true.

What is real and true is what is here, now. What is your experience in this moment? What are you seeing, hearing, feeling, smelling, tasting, and sensing, including what you may be sensing on more subtle levels: love, gratitude, peace, compassion, joy, excitement, strength, courage, an intuition, an insight, an inspiration, an urge, an impulse, a drive? These experiences are all you know for sure about your corner of the universe.

Pretending to know things beyond your actual experience in the here and now that cannot be known is not helpful. What possible value could pretending to know something have? It is not helpful to pretend that you know what's going to happen next year or even tomorrow—because you don't know for sure. That's the truth. It is not helpful to pretend to know what someone is thinking or what someone will or will not do, or even what you will do—because you don't know for sure. That's the truth. It is also not helpful to pretend to know why something happened. That is especially hard to know, because as we have seen, there is an incalculable number of possible causative factors for any event. The truth is *you don't know very much for certain—and you don't need to know.*

One might argue that you need to pretend to know that a meeting that is scheduled for tomorrow will take place, or you won't get there. But that isn't even true. If a meeting is scheduled, you would prepare for it and do whatever you needed to do to attend it but still realize that it might not take place. You aren't pretending to know that it will take place but simply preparing for the likelihood that it will, barring nothing interfering with that.

Such practical matters are still taken care of when you are in touch with the truth about life. It's just that if the meeting doesn't happen and you didn't pretend it was going to happen, you are less likely to feel upset because you won't tell yourself, "That meeting should have happened!" Instead, you'll go with the flow: "Ah yes, life doesn't always go as planned." And that's the truth.

This pretending to know isn't even conscious. It's more like you truly believe you know something without realizing you don't and without questioning it. That is the nature of an illusion. Many of the thoughts in the thought-stream are like this. They make you feel like you know more than you do. However, pretending to know and knowing are completely different. Pretending belongs to the imagination, and as useful and enjoyable as the imagination can be, when it is used to pretend to know what cannot be known, it takes one out of reality and more deeply into the Illusion.

The thoughts about the past and future are of a similar nature: They are imaginations. You imagine the past as you think it was, and you imagine the future as you hope or fear it will be. How useful is this? All that is left of the past is a memory, and memories are not real nor generally very accurate. And fantasies, by definition, are not real. Memories and fantasies are thoughts that don't represent anything real.

Do you need your thoughts about the past and the future? You need them to create an imaginary reality for the imaginary you to live in. The story about the me's past, present, and future is the illusory reality in which the *me* lives. All made up.

The Illusion is called that for a reason. It is something that seems other than what it actually is. Isn't that what an illusion is? You see a patch of wetness ahead on the road, but it isn't what it seems to be. The water you think you see is a mirage, an illusion. It seems real, but it isn't. The illusory world created by the egoic mind seems real, but it isn't. The imaginary you seems real, but it isn't.

The most convincing feature of the Illusion is the illusion of *you*. In fact, the purpose of the Illusion is to create and maintain this imaginary you. It gives the *you* a description, identities, self-images, a history, stories, problems to solve, desires to pursue, dreams to dream, fears to fear. It even gives the *you* feelings. The stories, problems, fears, and desires cause the *you* to feel a variety of feelings.

Those feelings drive actions and shape behavior in the real world. The Illusion affects reality, which makes the Illusion seem even more real. If your internal world had no relation to the real world, you would be considered insane, delusional. But the Illusion involves the real world.

Everyone is sharing in the same Illusion, so it hardly seems like an illusion. If no one is aware that something is an illusion, is it still an illusion? Then it would appear to be reality, even though it would be more like a shared dream. This is the situation in which humanity finds itself, in this world shaped by people's egos. The reality created by the egoic state of consciousness seems like how reality actually is—but it isn't! Now, that is a great illusion!

This means that the beliefs that egos share are thought to be true by most people: "You have to struggle to survive. It's a dog-eat-dog world. You have to look out for #1. There's never enough time. There isn't enough to go around. People can't be trusted. Money equals happiness." This also means that the reality created by those beliefs becomes the reality most people live in. People are living in a world shaped by egoic beliefs, values, perceptions, and behaviors. The Illusion is made manifest in your world! It has coopted reality.

But reality is still there, of course. Although it is hidden by the Illusion, reality can be accessed in any moment by simply giving your attention to something real rather than something that is being produced by the Illusion.

What is real are the sensory and other more subtle experiences in the here and now. What is not real are imaginations, pretenses of knowing, memories, fantasies, wishes, dreams, desires, self-images, identities, stories, beliefs, and fears. That's a lot that isn't real! Well, you need a lot of ideas and feelings that stem from those ideas to make an illusion seem real. On the other hand, reality is quite simple.

The imaginary you—the egoic self—doesn't actually like simple. Without all the thoughts, desires, and feelings that make up the Illusion, the imaginary you could not exist. So to say that it likes the world of thoughts, desires, and feelings is an understatement. The imaginary you needs these to survive.

As long as you perceive yourself as the *you* who has dreams, desires, fears, self-images, stories, beliefs, and so forth, you will be more interested in the egoic mind's illusory world than the real world. Reality, the world of the senses and the subtle world, is not of much interest to the mind-generated *you,* which loves the drama created by thoughts and feelings. But there is another *you* here.

That *you* is the one I am speaking to and the one who is reading this. Isn't that funny that we can talk about you this way? It's like we are talking about you behind your back. We are talking about the illusory you behind its back. We can do that because it is imaginary. Notice how it can't talk about the real you behind its back! It doesn't work the other way around because the imaginary you can't perceive the truth about itself, since it doesn't exist and it isn't what perceives.

What perceives the truth about the imaginary you is the real you. Hello there! How nice to have you here. Welcome to your awakening, to waking up to the truth about life. You are receiving the Truth on an intellectual level right now, but many of you are also getting a glimpse, a realization, of it too, since a realization is only a little step away from an intellectual understanding.

There is no end to the depth to which the Truth can be realized. At whatever depth you are realizing it, that is the right experience, and that will take you to the next level. Although you can't really skip levels, you might move through some levels very quickly. You don't have to worry about how realization unfolds, however, because something very wise is in charge of "your" realization, and it is also benevolent.

Just as the imaginary reality created by the thought-stream seems real, the imaginary you created by thoughts and feelings seems like the real you. And other people's self-images and your images of them seem like who they really are too (even though these could be vastly different).

This wouldn't be so much of a problem if the imaginary you were more like the real you, but they are nearly opposite:

❖ *The imaginary you is afraid of life, while the real you loves and embraces life.*

❖ *The imaginary you distrusts life and itself, while the real you trusts life and trusts the flow of life through itself.*

❖ *The imaginary you is guarded and closed toward others, while the real you is open and loving.*

❖ *The imaginary you is judgmental, while the real you is accepting and forgiving.*

❖ *The imaginary you is self-centered, while the real you knows there is no personal self that needs anything.*

❖ *The imaginary you feels lacking and inadequate, while the real you knows it has access to everything needed to flourish and be happy.*

❖ *The imaginary you lacks the love, compassion, courage, inner strength, patience, wisdom, and clarity that define the real you.*

❖ *The imaginary you produces negative emotions, while the real you produces love, peace, gratitude, joy, courage, strength, patience, compassion, kindness, inspiration, and wisdom.*

❖ *The imaginary you feels unworthy and not good enough, while the real you accepts and forgives its own imperfections and mistakes and is not defined by them. The real you recognizes that making mistakes and learning from them is how progress is made.*

The *you* that many traditional religions reflect back to you, the *you* they believe you to be, is more like the imaginary you than the real you. To the degree that religions do this, they reinforce and maintain the Illusion. They see you as separate from God and fail to recognize that God resides in you. They assume that who you are is your egoic self, which keeps you (and themselves) in a prison of limitation, inadequacy, fear, guilt, and distrust in one's own power. That may be to their advantage in maintaining their own hierarchy and power, but it is not to your advantage to see yourself this way.

To their credit, religions do encourage people to aspire to be more like their true self. However, most religions don't offer a very effective way for becoming that beyond telling people what *not* to do. Few religions offer the types of spiritual practices that enable people to experience their true nature, because they don't even see this as a goal.

Believing that this imaginary you—the one who feels lacking, unworthy, fearful, and distrusting—is who you really are is problematic because such a *you* is not very effective in the world, unless you become the other possibility, one that religions suggest you not become: someone who is selfish, greedy, ruthless, and power-hungry. Either way, this imaginary you stands little chance of finding true happiness or love.

If this is how you feel about yourself, love doesn't easily flow toward others or to yourself. The irony is that love—the very thing religions tout—is blocked by the image of yourself as sinful, unworthy, flawed, weak, distrusting, and frightened. And, of course, love is also blocked by the opposite persona: selfish, greedy, ruthless, and power-hungry.

The real problem is that believing you are this imaginary you makes it hard to believe you are the real you and the qualities exemplified by that. How do you move from believing you are the imaginary you to knowing who you really are?

Even if it wanted to, the imaginary you can't help you discover who you really are—because it is imaginary! The only thing that can help you discover this is the real you. It is the only thing that has ever done anything in your life, including pretend to be the imaginary you.

To move from the imaginary you to the real one, you have to have some experience of the real you. For that, you have to have seen through the Illusion at least a little bit. That happens when the real you begins to wake up within you. This is a mysterious and momentous event in one's spiritual evolution, which many only become aware of when they find themselves questioning life more deeply. This often lands them on the spiritual path, where they hopefully can get help moving from the imaginary you to the real you.

Traditional religions and self-help programs, on the other hand, generally try to help people move from the imaginary you to a better version of this imaginary you, one that is happier, more gentle and kind, and more successful. However, if you still believe you are sinful and unworthy, these efforts are like trying to pull yourself up by your own bootstraps. The imaginary you can learn to feel better about itself and behave better, but its basic identity will always be that of someone who is flawed and lacking.

The imaginary you can become happier, kinder, and more successful by taking on new beliefs and self-images that are more aligned with the true self. This is a common stepping stone and often pokes enough of a hole in the Illusion to allow people to realize who they really are more clearly, which is not an idea or an image but an *experience*. There is a big difference between believing you are loving and good and experiencing the self that *is* love and goodness. Nevertheless, the belief in your innate goodness is often the bridge to the experience of who you really are.

The shift to believing you are loving and good is able to be made by recognizing that self-images such as flawed, bad, unworthy, inadequate, and not good enough are not true and then affirming the opposite. This reprogramming of mistaken beliefs and self-images is how the spell of the Illusion is ultimately broken. Affirming that you have the qualities of the true self opens the door to experiencing who you really are and the very qualities you have been affirming.

But make no mistake, the new, healthier, happier self-image is not who you really are. It only makes discovering who you are easier. This healthier self-image can still be corrupted by the ego. For instance, your happier, more successful imaginary you might conclude that you are now better than others because you have figured out how to "manifest" success through confidence and a more positive attitude. But that is still not the true self, only just another, more functional, self-image.

The experience of who you are doesn't turn you into someone special but, instead, eliminates any sense of specialness the ego might have enjoyed. It also wipes out egoic drives that push people to be successful for the sake of success alone. Realizing who you really are changes everything. You can't get lost in the Illusion in the same way anymore. This makes you different from others, which can be challenging. You don't fit in like you used to, but that doesn't matter to you. You are content and not looking for anything outside yourself to make you happy.

The most miraculous thing about this state of consciousness, which is your natural state, is that it enables you to accept life just as it is and see the good in it. You are no longer a struggling, lacking person up against a fearful world, where the odds are stacked against you. Instead, you feel more like the child of an abundant and loving Father, who has given you everything you need to survive and be happy.

In this state of consciousness, it is easy to see the truth about life: its goodness, beauty, and support. Once you see this, then that goodness and bounty become more available to you. What you believe to be true about reality becomes your reality. If you believe in a world that is against you, then that will be your experience. If you believe in a world that is supportive, then that will be your experience.

The proof of this is that the experience of life in the egoic state of consciousness is primarily one of strife and suffering, while the experience of life in your natural state is one of Grace. And yet, reality has not changed at all—only your perception of it. When you change your beliefs, your experience of reality changes. The fact is that reality has always been the way it is: good, supportive, and plentiful. It's just that most people don't recognize this.

So let's talk about when bad things happen. First of all, "bad" is a perception, a point of view, which is not the perspective of the true self. "Bad" is a concept, a mental construct, which turns experiences, people, and things into one of two possibilities: good or bad. These are very broad categories! Nevertheless, this is how the ego sees things and how the thought-stream presents things: Something is either good or bad. It is either something "I" like or don't like, or something "I" want or don't want.

This way of seeing things results in feelings: "If I get something I like, I'm happy. If I get something I don't like, I'm unhappy. If something bad happens, I'm mad. If something good happens, I can finally be happy and relax." Given that people aren't in control of what happens to them, that doesn't leave many moments for happiness.

One of the reasons those who are awakened or enlightened are happy, or at least not unhappy, no matter what happens is that they don't believe their mind's assessment of good or bad. Who's to say something is good or bad? Life isn't that simple. Experiences have both desirable and undesirable aspects. *The only thing in life that is black or white are those colors. There is a positive side to every negative experience and vice versa.* This is another truth about life. The trouble with thinking an experience is bad is that you're likely to overlook what is good about it.

Granted, some experiences are less desirable than others, but that doesn't mean they shouldn't be happening, which is the ego's assumption: "This shouldn't be happening, because I don't want it to!" The ego is egocentric, like a child. The ego doesn't want life to be the way it is, because it wants life to be the way it wants life to be. But life isn't! Life is the way it is regardless of how you feel about it. Throwing a tantrum about it doesn't change anything. Tantrums only make you suffer. *When you don't accept the way life is, you suffer.* This is another truth about life.

Taking the ego's point of view results in suffering because the ego's perspective is incomplete and therefore untrue. When you believe a lie, life will show you it is a lie by causing you internal distress: suffering. That's how benevolent life is. Even suffering isn't bad. It might feel bad, but its purpose is good: to point you away from your narrow, incomplete perspective to a truer, more complete one. Through suffering, life is trying to tell you something. Your job is to discover what that is. You are here to learn from life.

Those who are happy have learned this truth about life: *Life is a school. Your experiences are your teachers. You are here to learn and grow.* Life is not about getting your way. When you accept what life brings you, which you have no control over, you can be happy, or at least not suffer. The ego doesn't see it this way. It sees life as something to conquer. It wants something it can never have: control. The ego doesn't see the truth about life but tries to make life fit its "truth," or the lie it tells itself about having control.

The problem with pretending you have control over life is that when life shows you that you don't by bringing you something you don't want, you feel humiliated. You feel like *you* have failed. Your imaginary self feels defeated by life, and it takes that defeat very personally. It suffers over not being good enough to have been able to control life. It suffers because it doesn't accept that it doesn't have control.

Those who don't suffer over so-called bad things happening also realize that what happens in life isn't personal. "Bad" things happening is not proof that *you* are bad, unworthy, sinful, or being punished, as religions have sometimes implied. To the extent that religions have suggested this, they do a great disservice to people. In failing to adequately explain why so-called bad things happen or by offering explanations that fall short of the truth, they perpetuate people's suffering.

Difficult things happen; wonderful things happen. They are all part of the play, the cards that are dealt. Those who don't suffer over what is happening realize that there is no other choice that makes sense but to say yes to whatever is happening. Fighting with life or being unhappy with life or blaming yourself for what has happened is useless.

Surrendering to what is, is the key to happiness. Accepting what is happening or has happened simply means accepting that it is happening or has happened even if your egoic self is not happy with it. Interestingly, acceptance and resistance can be going on simultaneously within you. Your egoic self, through the thought-stream, may be resisting and complaining about what it doesn't like. But let it. It doesn't matter what your thought-stream is spewing or stewing about, because you know that the *you* that is resisting life is imaginary. You are the one who is in touch with the deeper truth about life: *Everything is unfolding as it needs to.*

Just as it wouldn't bother you if someone you didn't know was spewing and stewing about something, you don't have to be bothered by your own thoughts. They are meaningless, and they are no more yours than someone else's. They are just the conditioning you were given. Once you know that, your thoughts lose their power to make you suffer.

So much of the pain in life comes from the resistance, anger, fear, and sadness stemming from one's attitude about what is happening, not actually from events. The unpleasant feelings that tend to accompany so-called bad things make things feel much worse than they need to. People cause their own suffering without even realizing their role in that.

Whatever is happening that you don't like is happening in one moment of time and unfolding one moment at a time. If you stay with that unfolding and don't jump forward in time or backward, you won't create any unpleasant feelings, and you will be able to deal with the situation more wisely. On the other hand, feelings take you out of the moment-to-moment flow of life and keep you in the ego's imaginary reality, where "bad" seems very true and problematic and where your inner wisdom is less accessible.

The good news is you can avoid creating such feelings by simply accepting the truth about the situation: *Whatever is happening is what life in your corner of the universe is all about for you for now.* Accepting the situation in this way allows you to stay present, which enables you to take advantage of the wisdom, strength, courage, perseverance, and patience you are being given to deal with the situation. The truth is *you always have whatever you need to deal with whatever life brings you.* You have been endowed with all the necessary internal resources, and Grace will bring you whatever else you might need from the external world.

If you understand that whatever is happening is meant to be happening, then so-called bad things can be accepted and understood to be serving some purpose. At the very least, difficulties stretch you and force you to develop your inner resources, enabling you to become stronger, wiser, more patient, more responsible, or whatever else you are meant to become as a result of that challenge. Difficulties make you a better person because to deal with them, you have to summon the best parts of yourself or you will suffer. Your challenges evolve you and uncover the goodness that has always been there. They help you discover the truth about yourself.

People grow in their strengths by having to call on those strengths:

❖ *You become courageous by having to face your fears.*

❖ *You become patient or persevering by being tried.*

❖ *You become responsible by being given responsibilities.*

❖ *You become compassionate by experiencing a lack of compassion from others.*

❖ *You become able to control your anger by being angered.*

❖ *You discover strength because strength is demanded.*

❖ *You develop endurance because endurance is demanded.*

❖ *You become wise by first being foolish.*

❖ *You gain understanding by first misunderstanding.*

When you are being challenged, you discover that taking anything but the "high road" only leads to more suffering. So your capacity to walk the high road, to move in a way that is aligned with the Truth, develops. Suffering is your wise and patient teacher. This teacher will deliver suffering for as long as it takes for you to learn to go in the direction of the Truth, the direction of love, peace, and harmony.

In this world, suffering is pure kindness. It is showing you the way in the only way possible in a world that is designed to evolve through suffering. And, of course, the greatest kindness is that you are released from suffering when you are finally willing to choose the Truth.

Difficulties are also an opportunity to learn something — and learn it fast usually. There is nothing like pain to speed along one's learning. For this reason, souls sometimes choose extremely challenging experiences. They want to speed through their lessons — skip grades. Dealing with very painful situations is one way to do that. Your soul has chosen to come into this world to grow. You may wish it were otherwise, but your soul doesn't. The more you are onboard with that, the easier your challenges will be.

Your attitude toward your circumstances is so important. With the right understanding and attitude, bad things are not bad and suffering can be minimized. Learning how to not suffer is one of the most important lessons you will learn in this school called life.

Without the right understanding and attitude, people suffer greatly, but even that is the right experience. Extreme suffering often wakes people up out of their usual egoic perceptions and motivates them to seek help or ask important questions, which often leads to the Truth. So how bad, really, are bad things?

In addition to not seeing life in terms of good and bad, another reason that those who are awakened or enlightened are happy, or at least not unhappy, no matter what happens is that they don't require that circumstances make them happy. They don't need events, people, things, or experiences to feel happy because they are already happy. Being in touch with their true nature is enough.

Everyone is searching for happiness, and it is your birthright to be happy. Your natural state is one of happiness, peace, and contentment. What the search for happiness reveals is that lasting happiness is not found outside yourself but within you. I realize this sounds trite, as all truisms do because they are so often repeated; and yet, how many really understand what it means to find happiness within?

Inner happiness is a subtle, energetic experience of joy that is not based on anything specific but is simply the joy that your being feels in existing. Just that. This joy is so subtle that unless you have cultivated your subtle senses, you are likely to overlook it much of the time. But the more attuned you become to this joy, the more available it is.

This inner happiness doesn't feel like the usual happiness because it is not the same as the happiness of the ego. There's nothing wrong with the ego's happiness, which comes from getting what the ego wants. It feels wonderful, and it is meant to feel wonderful. It is Grace. It is a gift. It's just that this type of happiness doesn't last, and if you think it should or you want it to last, you will suffer when it leaves.

Enjoy that happiness while you can, knowing that it will pass and be replaced by other feelings, because the nature of feelings is that they come and go. That ephemeral happiness doesn't have to be replaced by suffering as long as you accept its transitory nature and understand that that kind of happiness is not meant to be anyone's ongoing experience.

No one is happy in that way all the time. To believe that that kind of happiness can be constant is a fantasy. So if you don't feel wonderful all the time, just know that it is not your fault. It isn't proof of your unworthiness or inadequacy.

The happiness of the Heart is very different, so different that it deserves another name. Some people do call it by another name: joy. Joy is subtle but beautiful. It is quiet, unlike the ego's bouncy happiness. You know what joy feels like. When you feel it, that is your being rejoicing in life, which it is always doing.

Joy is always happening, like an underlying hum that accompanies life. Joy is always available, but you might have to tune in to it before you may notice it. It is the same joy of the flower as it opens to the sun, the leaves as they blow in the wind, the rain as it falls from the sky. It is the joy of all life doing whatever it is doing, whatever it was born to do. The Divine is always rejoicing, in a never-ending song to life. This is who you are. You are this simple joy in existing.

From this place of joy, flow love, peace, and wisdom. Your instructions for how to live your life come from this same subtle realm in which joy exists. This joy is there to guide your life. If you listen to it, you will not only be joy-full, but also happy in the usual sense more often. This joy beckons you to a happy life, which is possible if you are living the life you are meant to live according to the grand design. This is another reason why those who are aligned with their true self are happy: They are in harmony with their soul's plan.

Another reason that everyone has difficulties, even those who are in harmony with life, is that some worlds, such as your own, are designed to evolve through challenges. Your world is one among many that has both a positive and a negative pole. Love is the positive pole, and fear is love's opposite, the negative pole.

In such worlds there are difficulties, or challenges, and suffering over those difficulties until suffering is conquered. Always, there is given a way out of suffering, including saviors and other means. The Designer has no intention of becoming lost in suffering or lost in creation. A way out of a particular Illusion and the suffering caused by that is built in to every Illusion.

Not all worlds are designed to be difficult, however. Just as you might go to a spa purely for pleasure and relaxation, some worlds are designed for ease and recuperation. Every soul has many experiences on such worlds. But your soul is also likely from time to time in this infinite and eternal creation to enjoy testing its mettle fighting dragons or corporate greed or environmental degradation, and then you visit a world that offers that, such as yours (except for the dragons).

Because you forgot that you chose this type of world, it may seem like you are being punished, but that is far from the truth. Your soul specifically chose this world because this planet at this point in time can serve your evolution most elegantly. So one answer to why bad things happen, even to good people, is simply that their souls chose to have those experiences and chose to be born into a world that evolves through suffering.

There is one other question that deserves answering: "Why does life seem so unfair at times?" It often appears that the people doing bad things get away with it at the expense of others, who are doing their best to be good. Many even seem to be rewarded for their bad behavior and greed. You wonder: "Is God paying attention or doing anything about this?" You feel left alone, like being in a classroom with a lot of naughty children and no teacher to discipline them. You feel at the mercy of lawlessness and greed. Where is the justice, you wonder?

One of the lessons humanity is learning is to define right and wrong and create laws that work for society. This is one of your challenges. How do you, as human beings, make society work? You discover this by seeing what doesn't work and then trying to fix that or adjust that through rules and laws. You are meant to devise laws that are aligned with and support the Truth.

You are meant to learn to deliver justice yourself, not that there isn't also a higher justice—karma—at work. However, the workings of karma are not necessarily apparent to you, which is another reason justice may seem to be lacking in your world. Karma is the Great Teacher, and it is working behind the scenes to bring about everyone's evolution in a very wise and measured way. It bears mentioning that karmic circumstances are designed to teach, not punish, which is something that is often misunderstood about karma.

Life on planet Earth is a messy business of learning through trial and error. In that sense, although you are never alone, you are left to work things out on your own, just as you might leave a child alone with a new puzzle to figure it out. You know the child will eventually figure it out because you trust the child's intelligence, which he or she inherited from you.

Your intelligence knows what the child can handle, and so it is with the Designer, who has given you the resources you need to solve your own problems. That is what you are here to do: learn, grow, develop, create, love, and serve the Whole with your intelligence, your courage, and the other resources you have been given.

Everyone is learning, and everyone's teacher is suffering. There are other gentler teachers as well: books, healers, spiritual teachers, lovers, friends, and other helpers. But the process of learning is such that people make mistakes and, in so doing, hurt or harm others. It can be no other way. You are given an ego that creates an illusory reality, which doesn't reflect the Truth, and you are meant to discover the Truth. It is discovered by following the faulty programming until it causes so much pain for yourself and others that you wake up out of the programming and find another way to live.

If you see the mistakes that others make along the way as unfair, then that is an opportunity to change your perception to one that doesn't make you suffer. Seeing life as bad or unfair or people as bad or unfair is not helpful, because it makes you suffer. Find a way to see things that doesn't cause you pain, and you will have found the Truth. Other people are your teachers in this way. They challenge you to find a way to not suffer over their behavior.

Life seems unfair to the ego because the ego wants life to be a certain way. But life isn't unfair. It is the way it is for a reason, and that reason is not unreasonable or unkind or unfair. It is the way it is so that you will awaken from the Illusion and discover the glory of your divine nature. Everyone's story has a happy ending.

CHAPTER 5

Qualities of the Truth

The truth about life is revealed in a more subtle realm than your ordinary consciousness, which is dominated by thoughts and sensory input. By exploring the qualities of the Truth, such as love and peace, this chapter will help you become more acquainted with the subtle realm, with reality.

This won't be very appealing to the mind, however, because from its perspective, the subtle realm is too "unreal" to be of much interest. The mind is fascinated by the sensory world and even more so by its own imaginary world, but not so much by reality.

To the mind, saying, "Let's explore the subtle realm" is like saying, "Let's explore the dust on the moon." The aspects of this subtler realm seem no more distinct to the mind than one particle of moon dust is from another: "Moon dust is moon dust. It all looks the same to me. Love is love. What's the big deal?"

But, of course, anyone who is truly curious, such as a scientist or an explorer, would love to get his or her hands on moon dust. You, too, have an Inner Explorer who is curious about this hidden dimension of life we are calling the Truth.

This is interesting, isn't it, that you can be curious about something that your mind is not? In fact, the mind is the hurdle in this exploration.

Who or what is this *you* that is curious? It turns out that curiosity is one of the qualities of the Truth! Curiosity comes from your being. It is a form of love, an expression of love for creation.

The mind assumes it knows what love, peace, joy, gratitude, curiosity, and strength are because it has words for them. Words make these seem like distinct things, while they are actually different qualities of the same thing. Just as every color of the rainbow is a different radiation of the same thing—light—love, peace, joy, gratitude, curiosity, and strength are different radiations of the Truth. The Truth has other qualities as well.

The Truth is the underlying reality, the substratum of creation. However, to say that the Truth underlies creation makes it seem separate from life, while it isn't. The Truth cannot be separated out from life because it is life. It is the very Consciousness that created life and which is experiencing it. To say that the Truth interpenetrates life would be more accurate, but that is still misleading.

Although the Truth is challenging to describe, it is the most common experience. No one has not experienced the Truth, because it is all that is here. Without the Truth, there would be no experience. Therefore, a better name for the Truth, which many do use, might be Consciousness or Awareness. You could say that the Truth is conscious. It is the Consciousness that gave birth to life, is infused in life, and experiences life.

Just as water can be described by its qualities, such as wetness and colorlessness, Consciousness can be described by its qualities, even though those descriptions will naturally always fall short. The particular qualities of the Truth that we are going to explore are love, peace, gratitude, and strength. Let's look first at love, which I've already said quite a bit about

If you could use only one word to describe the Truth, it would be love. It comes closest to the nature of Consciousness, the nature of life, and the nature of the Designer (which are all the same thing). Love is the motivating and attractive force behind all life, which exists because love created and sustains it. If it were not for love, nothing would exist.

This is true in your life as well: As above, so below. To use a simple example, if people didn't love cookies, they wouldn't have created them or continue creating them. If they didn't love being warm, they wouldn't have created clothing. If they didn't love expressing themselves, they wouldn't have created interesting clothing.

Look around you and simply notice all that you love and acknowledge that you or someone else created those things out of love. Even if someone else created them, you chose to own them. What chose? Your love for something about it chose it.

What would it be like to look from eyes that recognize that everything that exists came from love and is sustained by love? What if this were your usual way of perceiving? What if every time you looked at something you *experienced* this love? This experience is your natural state and not really an experience at all, not a passing one anyway. You *are* the experience of life.

Love is the experience of your being in every moment. This is the love that underlies all life. Your being is loving life, loving existing, and loving experiencing what it has created. Once you realize this underlying reality exists, you can tune in to it wherever you choose. Experiencing the existence of this reality isn't difficult, but you have to want to and you have to choose to. Otherwise, you will continue perceiving in the way you usually do and overlook the subtle reality.

Over the course of your spiritual evolution, the subtle reality becomes increasingly more predominant in your awareness. Enlightenment is the experience of being in touch with the Truth in most moments. Although those who are enlightened may not be in touch with the Truth constantly, they never lose sight of its existence and can always return to the subtle realm by simply giving it their attention.

A certain capacity to experience the subtle realm must be developed. This is accomplished in the same way anything is: through practice. By turning your attention again and again to the subtle realm, as is done in meditation, your ability to perceive this realm and maintain that perception is improved. Like anything that must be practiced, just reading about this isn't enough. You have to practice giving your attention to something other than the usual thoughts and feelings.

Doing this is hard at first, like doing anything new. But the more you practice attending to the subtle realm, the easier it becomes. What you are doing by practicing this is creating connections in your brain that will make tuning in to the subtle realm more natural and automatic. Once these connections are developed, you will have "learned" how to do this. Then as long as you continue using this capability, you will retain it.

And why, you might ask, would you want to develop a greater sensitivity to the subtle realm? Your mind isn't interested in this, but something else is, which is waking up in you and moved to know itself more fully. At a certain point in your spiritual evolution, you become curious about knowing who you really are and what is really going on. Your love flows toward the Truth, and you are no longer so interested in how you look and how much you have in your bank account. Other things, deeper things, begin to matter more than what the ego has been so attracted and attached to.

This is mysterious, isn't it? How does this evolution happen? It just happens, doesn't it? You didn't cause it or make it happen. Just as a flower naturally blossoms, so do you. You are designed to bloom spiritually at a particular time. You could say that you are programmed to awaken to your true nature. However, this is not programming of the usual sort, but more like programming intended to disrupt or transform the programming!

Love loves the character, and it also loves waking up from the character. What fun! Love is that excitement, that joy in experiencing something new, that sense of fun. Everything that feels good within you—peace, happiness, excitement, fun, curiosity, gratitude, strength, clarity—is love. Every good feeling you can possibly name or experience is a flavor of love.

Stop for just a moment and let yourself feel what love feels like. It's easy to experience it. If you can't find it right away, simply remember a time when you felt love. This is an excellent use of memory. Then notice specifically how love feels in your body. Notice the subtle energy of love. Notice how it registers in your subtle energy body. Love is an energetic experience! This is the subtle realm.

You can sooth yourself and shift your consciousness whenever you want by simply focusing on the energetic experience of love or calling love forth by remembering it. Looking at certain pictures or videos, like of sunsets or puppies, and listening to uplifting music can also evoke love. And, of course, there are your favorite foods and things like cozy blankets and other comforts to help you remember love. The more you bring your attention to such things, to the love that already exists in your environment, the easier it will be to evoke love in more challenging situations. Evoking love and being with the energy of love in this way is a very valuable spiritual practice.

An example that illustrates the difference between the mind's perceptions and the Heart's might be helpful. Take a bridge, for instance. What a marvel a bridge is! It was built just for you and also by you, from the greater perspective. It took everything up to now to create it and sustain it. It was not only designed with love and born from love, but also used and maintained with love. This is how your Heart sees a bridge, although much more could be said about a bridge from the Heart's perspective than just this.

The mind sees a bridge quite differently, and none of its perceptions includes the ones just mentioned. Instead, the mind sees a bridge and thinks: "It's old. It could collapse—and then what would happen? That would be a terrible death, plunging into the water. How did they build this thing? I hate driving over bridges. I can't look down. I heard they paid way too much for it. What a waste of taxpayers' money! The corruption in this city is awful." All of those thoughts might come within seconds of each other. And to what purpose?

This last question is especially important, because if you don't examine such thoughts, they will seem normal, non-problematic, and even possibly useful. And from the mind's perspective, they are all true—you wouldn't want that bridge to collapse while you were on it! You might even think that that thought keeps you safe, but does it really?

The truth about such thoughts is that, on examination, you can't find a single one that serves you, and every one of them keeps you in a contracted state, divorced from the Heart's perceptions, which feel wonderful. If you had a choice, which thoughts would you choose: your Heart's or your mind's? Once you realize that an alternative to the mind's perceptions exists, you do have a choice.

Shifting from the mind to the Heart's perceptions is a powerful and empowering act that will change your life. By shifting your perception of reality, your experience of reality changes as well as that of those around you. The Heart's perspective not only is true and feels good, but also helps everyone around you begin to shift and feel better too.

The Heart's way is practical too, because when you feel good and contribute to the well-being of others, life goes more smoothly. Here's why:

❖ *You are less stressed and more present;*

❖ *More of your energy and intelligence are at your disposal;*

❖ *You make wiser choices and fewer mistakes;*

❖ *You are more easily guided intuitively; and*

❖ *You are more accepting, more loving, more compassionate, more creative, and more fun.*

Can you say anything like that about the mind's perceptions? They result in the opposite, don't they?

When I say "mind," I'm not referring to your intelligence, your capacity for rational thought, which is available to both the Heart and the ego. The mind I'm referring to is the egoic mind, the voice in your head. This voice is not the voice of your intelligence but the voice of the ego, a primitive survival-oriented aspect of yourself, which actually doesn't serve your survival very well, at least not in today's world.

The intelligence that is alive in you knows how to build that bridge. Now, that is useful! But love is ultimately what created the bridge. Without love, there would be no bridge.

Love used your intelligence to create it. Love is the hand of God, while you could say, your intelligence is the tool in that hand. Of course, your intelligence is also love, along with everything else you can see, feel, or name. It is all a gift, created from the very substance of God, by God, for God. And this God is, in a word, love.

This love is behind everything and drives everything. Take the beautifully patterned rug you walk on every day: Who cared for and sheared the sheep whose wool was used? Who carefully dyed and carded the wool? What plants were cultivated to make the dye? Who thoughtfully chose the colors? Who painstakingly designed the pattern and wove the wool? Who cleverly invented the loom? What tree gave its life for the loom? Whose sweat delivered the rug to the shipyard? Who spent weeks on the ship that carried it across the ocean? Who risked their lives drilling the oil used to transport it? Who dreamed the business into being that sold it? Who gave birth to all who were involved? What and who made it possible for them to survive long enough to do all this? It took all of creation and everything that ever happened to bring that rug into being and for it to be exactly as it is.

Everything is interconnected and interdependent, and what connects everything and what everything depends on is love. If you take love out of the picture, which would be impossible, your world would fall apart. It wouldn't work. Your world works to the extent that love is operating behind the scenes.

You see this in your world today: things not working well and people suffering as a result, because the mind's perceptions hold sway over the Heart's. When the mind's perceptions rule, the interconnectivity of life is overlooked or unappreciated. You lose touch with what is real and true about life, with your essence, with what is important, and with what can make you truly happy.

When that happens, you feel empty, and that emptiness seeks to be filled through material acquisition and power. But trying to fix unhappiness by acquiring things and power is like trying to fill a bucket that has a hole in it: There will never be enough to fill it. So this is your world. People misperceive. Rather than address the cause of their suffering, which is their misperceptions, people try to make life fit their misperceptions, their desires. However, only the Truth can set one free from the ego's misperceptions.

The Truth that frees is not solely an intellectual understanding of the Truth, as important as that is, but a deeper realization of it, an actual experience of your true nature as love. And that is what I hope to help you with. I am here to help you see from the eyes of love.

So look around you. That table is not just a table; it has a Presence of its own. It has a consciousness of its own, an aliveness that is palpable for those whose subtle senses have been trained. Open to the possibility of experiencing the table as it is, here and now, without its label, without thinking of it as an inanimate object. Nothing is inanimate. Words take the life out of life. But life is called life because it is alive. Everything you experience is part of one living reality that is here for you and that is, in fact, you.

Science confirms the animate nature of life. At the atomic and subatomic level, everything is in constant motion: alive. And on this level, there are no differences, just atoms and subatomic particles doing what they do. Everything is made of the same stuff. If you go even deeper, what you find is Consciousness. All life is conscious: It lives, experiences, and delivers information back to the Creator and to the Whole of which it is a part.

What if you really knew this? How would that change how you perceive the many things you view as inanimate? Would you walk through life more gently? Would you feel more gratitude for everything?

Do you see how your beliefs about things influence your experience of them, how believing something is lifeless or inanimate makes it so in your imaginary reality and, therefore, becomes your experience of reality? What you believe becomes true to you, even if it is not. So this is what happens. Your beliefs make things true to you, and you experience the reality created by your beliefs, not reality as it actually is.

To experience life as it really is, you have to see reality as it really is. It is only in this way that you can be happy. Reality, just as it is, will make you happy! It is your imaginary reality that makes you unhappy. There is no unhappiness in reality, no unhappiness when you are in touch with the Truth. The Truth is good!

Without your imagination and mistaken ideas and beliefs, experiencing anything but love and the other qualities of the Truth would be impossible. You can only experience something else, such as fear and limitation (which is a concept), through your imagination, which you are given the free will to do.

You are the creator of your suffering. The only role God plays in this is to allow you to do that or, rather, to allow itself to do that, since you are not actually separate from God. God did not do anything to you. You created your imaginary reality yourself with the help of the ego and other programming. And, of course, there is no separate *you* that even did that, just God playing hide and seek with itself, which was made possible by the programming. There is no separate *you*, only God pretending to be you for a while. What fun!

Pretending is fun when you know you are pretending. When you discover the Truth, you see this—that you were pretending to be the character, pretending to be at odds with life, pretending you were alone, weak, limited, and afraid. If you were God (which you are), what else would you do for a challenge but choose to experience the opposite of the Truth? The Designer has created worlds upon worlds to explore the endless possibilities presented by the opposite of the Truth.

Peace is another quality of the Truth, another flavor of your true self. Everyone experiences peace, if only briefly. As you progress on the spiritual path, you experience increasing peace and equanimity. Life doesn't ruffle you as much. Things happen, you experience them, and then they are gone without leaving a trace. A sense of inner stillness and equanimity carry you along throughout your day.

In the egoic state of consciousness, the experience is very different: Things happen, and then you think about them. They stay in your imagination and possibly in your body as feelings. Whenever you think about what you are experiencing, you split off from reality and move into a virtual reality: the ongoing drama and saga of *you*, where the feelings generated by your thoughts act as evidence for what you are saying to yourself. The virtual reality is self-reinforcing, so much so that it is difficult to experience anything other than your story about reality!

Stories can never be peaceful because, by definition, a good story has drama, tension, conflict, problems, desires, fears, and other emotions. A good story at some point also happily resolves the tension. No one likes to be left hanging, incomplete, in suspense. And yet, people's own stories are bound to be ones in which there is little relief from drama, problems, and emotions. The happy ending never comes, except for a brief respite here and there before the next drama begins.

But life is not actually a drama. The character's life may be, but life is not. If there is a *you* in your experience of life, however, you will experience drama. But when the *you* drops away, you are in the Now, and *voila!* no drama. There can be no drama in the Now because there is no time. When there is no time, there is no story. When there is no story, there is no imaginary you. This is why there is peace and equanimity in the Now. In the simple experience of the moment, you find peace because there is no longer a *you* seeking happiness somewhere else.

Searching for something you can't find is frustrating and exhausting. And feeling there's something's missing that you need to find is unsettling, the opposite of inner stillness. This sense of never being able to rest or just *be* is the experience of the egoic state of consciousness and why there is so little peace in that state. There can be no peace if you believe you need something before you can be at peace.

This is the shell game the ego plays: Peace isn't here, so you have to look for it over there. Oops! It isn't there either. Keep looking! And so it goes. Peace is elusive in the egoic state of consciousness, because if you ever found it, you would no longer be in the egoic state of consciousness. That state is designed to be self-sustaining, so you won't find peace there. The ego doesn't want you to find it.

What is peace like? I could describe it, but you already know what it is and could describe it yourself. However, have you ever really explored the *experience* of peace? What is peace like on a subtle energetic level? When you are experiencing peace, how does it feel in your body? Where is it located? If you sit with that experience for a while, you will see that peace has a unique flavor. It doesn't "taste" the same as love.

To evoke peace, you only have to take a few slow, deep breaths and then be still for a few moments and imagine yourself beside a peaceful lake, in a quiet forest, or somewhere else that is still and quiet. Stillness and quiet are inherent in peace, so whenever your body is still and your mind is quiet, as in meditation, you invite the experience of peace.

Oneness, emptiness, nothingness, and non-motion are also descriptors befitting peace. Nothing is stirring because you experience nothing separate from you to stir it. Therefore, imagining yourself in a remote location, such as on a mountain top, where you feel totally alone and solitary also evokes peace. This aloneness is not loneliness but an all-one-ness, where you feel complete, whole, and at one with All That Is.

One of the most accessible qualities of the Truth is gratitude because there are so many opportunities in one's daily life to experience gratitude. You are constantly encountering things to be grateful for if you are willing to notice them. You can also simply bring to mind what you are grateful for while sitting quietly, which is an excellent practice. The choice to say "Thank you" to things, people, and other aspects of creation is a powerful act.

What makes expressing gratitude powerful is that it opens your Heart, and when your Heart is open, you feel happy! The reason this is so is that an open Heart allows love to flow from you to others and to the world. That flow of love is the ultimate act, your essential purpose as a human being. The most important thing you can do for yourself and for this world is to open that gate to love. Gratitude may be the best way to open your Heart because it is the easiest.

There are any number of ways to evoke gratitude. The simplest is to say "Thank you" to something or someone directly. You can thank the air, the trees, the rain, the sun, the soil, and the food you eat. And don't forget the farmers who grow the food, the truckers who haul it, the people who sell it to you, and so on. The interconnectedness and interdependence of all things means that everything is worthy of your gratitude. Every single thing you can name or think of and every single living being is cause for gratitude.

The beauty of gratitude is not only that there is so much to be grateful for, but that it doesn't matter what you are grateful for, since the effect is the same. Gratitude for a stone can open your Heart as easily as for your beloved or your child.

The Heart opens easily when you have that intention. Saying "Thank you" is an expression of that intention. It's like saying, "I choose to express gratitude now because I want love, peace, and joy to be my experience of life." Saying "Thank you" is an intention, a choice, for love and goodness.

One of the things that makes saying "Thank you" so easy is that you were trained to do it at certain times. Expressing gratitude is part of your conditioning! Many other niceties belong to your conditioning as well, like saying "Please" or signing letters "Sincerely" or "Warm Regards." Such conditioning exists because people recognized the power of love in obtaining support and cooperation and smoothing the way in life. This is something to be thankful for as well. Your conditioning is by no means all bad.

By practicing saying "Thank you" more often, you can condition yourself to be grateful more often. Saying "Thank you" to lots of things in your life, not just the usual things, can become a habit. Being grateful and loving can become a habit! Since feeling grateful and loving is what your true self is always doing, training your human self to feel gratitude and love more often will help you stay in touch with your true self.

A common method for evoking gratitude is to make a list of things you are grateful for. It's easiest to start with things your ego is grateful for: comforts, beautiful things, pets, loved ones, sunshine, a new car, a good job, a nice home, chocolate cake, a hot shower.

But what if you don't have those things? Can you still be grateful? Being grateful for what you *do* have will help you not suffer over what you don't have.

And can you be grateful even for your challenges and so-called problems, for the things your ego doesn't like but your true self welcomes?

The alternative is not accepting the way things are and suffering over that. Gratitude is a much better option. The more difficult the situation, the more necessary gratitude is, or you will struggle all the more. Challenges teach you this. They teach you how to be happy regardless of your circumstances. What a gift! What Grace.

Including more challenging things on the list of what you are grateful for is a particularly powerful thing to do. It's an excellent way of overcoming the ego's negativity and resistance to life. For instance, if you are dealing with a health issue, you might include:

❖ *I'm grateful for the opportunity to learn whatever I'm meant to learn from this.*

❖ *I'm grateful to discover what this experience will be like.*

❖ *I'm grateful for the doctors and nurses who are dedicated to helping me.*

❖ *I'm grateful there are possible solutions to this.*

❖ *I'm grateful I'm still capable of doing a lot of things.*

❖ *I'm grateful for all the body parts that still work.*

❖ *I'm grateful for the compassion and concern my friends and others have for me.*

❖ *I'm grateful I'm alive.*

❖ *I'm grateful I've had many years of good health.*

❖ *I'm grateful for the inner strength and wisdom to see things positively.*

This is "looking on the bright side" or "seeing the glass as half full," and it is the antidote to the egoic mind's perspective. This shift to focusing on the positives can make all the difference in one's experience of life. This is not pretending things are good when they aren't, but acknowledging the many things that *are* good even when some things aren't. This is seeing the *whole* truth about a situation, not just the ego's truth, not just the negative.

The advantage to seeing the whole truth is that it helps you cope by allowing you to access what you need to cope: compassion, acceptance, strength, patience, wisdom, insight, and forbearance. Being positive shifts your consciousness and makes it possible to tap into the inner resources you have been given to support you in this life.

In difficult times, the lesson often being taught and learned is greater strength. When you think of strength, you may think of endurance, perseverance, determination or physical strength. But what enables one to be strong and persevere is love: love for life or love for something or someone. Love is the force behind all kinds of strength and courage. Your greatest strength is the ability to love and be positive in the face of a challenge.

Without such challenges, people often don't realize just how strong they are or how much they love life or others. Challenges are an opportunity to overcome your fears and discover your resilience, courage, and love. They are an opportunity for the true self to step forward and for its qualities to be further developed and expressed through your human form. Not everyone discovers this, of course, but you have all of eternity!

Strength is another quality of the Truth. Strength is the willingness to adhere to and stand up for the Truth—for love, kindness, compassion peace, unity, acceptance, and tolerance. The ego fights in every possible way for what it *believes* to be right and true, while the true self stands strong for what is universally true, for the Truth. Learning the difference between the ego's truth and the Truth is one of life's lessons.

If life is founded on love, peace, and other qualities of the Truth, then these qualities must be what guide people's lives. When they don't, people behave in ways that go against life, which turns out badly for everyone. A world that lacks love and peace as guiding principles is not a world anyone would want to live in. That should be proof enough of the validity of these principles.

These universal principles are worth fighting for, but therein lies the rub. Do you go to war for the Truth? Do you kill people over love and peace? That makes sense only to the ego, in which case the ego's understanding of the Truth is distorted. The ego goes to war out of hatred or revenge, to get more of what it wants, or because it believes it needs to in order to survive or be safe. However, killing others for these reasons, even out of the *belief* that killing others will ensure your own survival or safety, is a bad strategy.

War only leads to more violence, hatred, and fear, the very things that made war seem necessary. Furthermore, going against life in this way takes a toll not only on those who suffer losses but on those who win, because killing is anti-life and anti-love. It takes a lot of rationalizing to make killing others okay within oneself. No one gains from war. Everyone loses.

Standing up for the Truth doesn't take place on a battlefield. It means living your life in such a way that love and peace are held more dear than egoic goals and values, if those goals and values conflict with the Truth. Standing up for the Truth means holding strong to compassion, love, peace, and acceptance — to goodness — in the face of forces that are moving against these values.

Wars may seem like they keep you safe, but it is love that does this, not might. Love builds societies and sustains them. Love is behind the cooperation that enables societies to flourish. The same would be true for the world if people could learn to cooperate with each other on a global scale.

War is an aberration, which one day your world will leave behind, although it is not ready to do so yet. War is not strength but weakness because it stems from fear and greed, which are weak positions. Fear and greed are a belief in lack and separation, a belief that there isn't enough to go around and that you have to fight to survive. This is the ego's point of view, and it is mistaken. Survival is supported and enhanced by cooperation, not conflict. Once humanity has learned this, you will stop fighting and start feeding each other.

Feeding and helping each other, caring for each other, having compassion for each other, accepting each other, loving each other, and doing the same for animals and the environment that support you is how you can best survive and flourish.

This is so simple a formula and so inherently rewarding and, yet, so difficult for the ego to implement. The ego is afraid to love and to give. It is afraid there won't be enough for itself, and it is afraid that kindness and generosity will make it vulnerable. As you would probably agree, this perspective is primitive and shortsighted.

Even if you are dedicated to love and peace, if those in power are not, you will live in a world of strife. Eventually, the Truth will win out, however, because it always does. Until then, do your best to stay true to love and peace, live by these principles, and stand up for them when necessary with your actions and speech, but not with violence.

Violence is never the way, even in today's uncertain world. "But, those with guns and nuclear weapons will kill us. We have to fight back," you say. That assumes that power comes from military might when it doesn't. Power comes from love. Love empowers you, it empowers others, and it attracts to you what you need. Furthermore, only love can change hearts and minds. You can't influence nations by fighting with them. You can't bully them into trusting you and cooperating with you. The opposite happens, and the hatred continues for generations. You know this. It is obvious, and yet, war continues because you believe it has to.

You are stronger than you think. However, this strength doesn't come from guns but from your capacity to join together and not yield to fear, war, and violence. If more people held strong to the principles of love and peace, sheer numbers could overcome the current mindset of fear, hatred, and greed and the maintenance of those values through violence.

War and violence hold sway because you allow them to, because you believe that the way it is, is the way it has to be. If you stopped believing this, the world would change. You would elect other people to office and not tolerate the cruelty perpetrated by some governments. You would give their people aide instead of guns and bombs. You would "kill them with kindness," as the saying goes. This works! It works among individuals, and it can work among nations as well. The key is to stop believing that war is necessary and start believing that war and violence must not be tolerated and that there is another way: love your neighbor.

If you are true to the principle of love, you will act accordingly: You will join together to withdraw support for the machinery of war. You will protest military actions and express your feelings about them to your representatives. You will work to elect people who do not support war. You will give aide to countries less fortunate than yours. You will tell your children that war is not acceptable or necessary. You will teach them there is another way: love.

If you argue that doing these things isn't enough, you're wrong. There are just not enough people doing them. Encourage people to join you in these actions. If enough people do these things, your world will change. It's just a numbers game. Too many people believe that war is necessary. When just as many people believe it isn't, you won't have it anymore. People are more powerful than they believe they are, but believing they are not powerful makes it so.

Your world is in transition from war to peace. You will either cause your own destruction or come through this period of trial. One promising trend is the exchange of commerce between nations. The more your business interests are intermingled with other countries, the less chance there is that you will destroy each other. This is one way that worlds similar to yours have made it through such transitions. It is a hopeful sign.

In these times, you have to summon the courage to love. Once you are aligned with love, you'll have the strength and courage to do whatever it takes to support love. You have to choose love above all else. That choice can only come from your true self, which is why a shift in consciousness is so important. How beautiful it is that you have stayed with this teaching this long. There is hope indeed.

As you move through the world and engage with others, you can practice evoking love and the other qualities of the Truth quite easily. Evoking any of the qualities of the Truth is a simple matter of turning your attention to the subtle experience of them in your body. Once you are very familiar with the energetic sensation of a quality of the Truth, you can find it and focus on it even when you are busy doing something in your home or out and about in the world. Focusing in this way brings you into the present moment and into Presence and anchors you there.

Focusing on a quality of the Truth, such as love, peace, gratitude, joy, or strength, gives your mind something to do, and that is important. If you don't consciously focus the mind, it will rattle on. The mind can only focus on one thing at a time, so if you are controlling its focus, then it cannot control you. You choose what your mind is doing, rather than the egoic mind determining what you do. This is the intent behind meditation and other spiritual practices, such as repeating a mantra or reciting a prayer.

If you are having difficulty tuning in to the subtle realm as you go about your day, focusing first on something less subtle, such as the breath, a sound, or sensations, can act as a bridge to the subtle realm. What are you seeing, hearing, tasting, smelling, or sensing? The body and senses can be used to bring you into the here and now and help you attune to the subtle realm. Then once you are experiencing peace, gratitude, or some other quality of the Truth, continuing to focus on that will bring you even more deeply into the subtle realm, more deeply into Presence.

CHAPTER 6

Life Is a School

One of the challenges in the school of life is that everyone isn't learning the same thing at the same time. Although all souls must eventually master the same lessons, each soul is working on different lessons and at a different level of mastery in those lessons. As a result, life is a little like a one-room schoolhouse. People are at different stages in their evolution and in different places of perception, and yet they have to find a way to work together and understand each other. This isn't always easy.

There are as many different points of view as there are people and all of them valid from their own perspective. A first grader's perspective is no less valid than a fifth grader's; they are just different points from which to view the world. Everyone's inner universe is valid for that person and therefore worthy of respect, and every perspective serves the evolution of the Whole. Tolerance is one of the lessons of life, and it is learned by encountering people very different from oneself.

Although challenging at times, this one-room schoolhouse is well designed for learning, since those who have already mastered what others haven't can teach them. In fact, this is an important feature of this design. And unlike school, in life, those farther along also learn from those less far along, who challenge them to grow in ways they might not otherwise grow. In the school of life, not only is life everyone's teacher, but everyone is everyone's teacher. So life is designed in such a way that *everyone is learning from everyone else. Everyone is learning, and everyone is teaching.* That is the truth.

Another feature of this school is that you are allowed to progress at whatever rate you choose. No one is pushing you to work harder or learn faster. Life is completely comfortable with you learning whatever you are learning at whatever pace you are learning it. There are so many lessons involved in life that you are bound to be learning something even if you aren't engaged in the particular lesson your soul intended. You cannot *not* learn in this school of life, so it is no problem how you go about that.

Without defining or describing this mysterious thing known as the soul, suffice it to say that everyone has one and everyone's soul has a loosely sketched out plan for this lifetime. This plan is often modified as choices are made and directions taken that don't match the original plan. Sometimes an intended lesson or life purpose is abandoned altogether in favor of one more suited to the circumstances created by the person's free will choices. Widely different choices than intended or expected are sometimes made, and then adjustments in the plan must be made.

Nevertheless, most people fulfill the intended lessons and life purpose to some extent and in some way. This is possible because of imprinting, or programming, which circumscribes and to some extent determines people's choices. For example, if your life purpose involves emergency work, such as police work, firefighting, or emergency medicine, then you will be programmed with a personality that suits that. Courageousness, assertiveness, strength, mental acuity, resiliency, tolerance of stress, and a desire to help others, all useful for emergency workers, are qualities people can be programmed to have. This type of person probably wouldn't be happy in a less demanding profession, while other personality types would be most unhappy doing emergency work. You are designed for a particular role, and programming ensures that you are suited to that role and attracted to it.

Each of you is unique, but you aren't responsible for that uniqueness. You don't decide one day to be the unique person you are, and you don't choose to be the way you are. You have to discover the special talents and qualities you have been given and then put them to use. You discover what they are because expressing them makes you happy. Through joy, your Heart shows you what your role and talents are.

People cannot be pigeon-holed into a profession or role just because they think they want to be in that role or because others, such as parents, want them to be. If people are in touch with their Heart, they would never want something other than what their Heart wants. When people want something other than that, it is because they are believing their ideas or other people's about who they should be. They don't realize that only their Heart knows what will fulfill them, not other people and not even their own mind. The problem is that knowing what the Heart wants is not something taught in schools, even though this is one of the most important lessons in the school of life.

What makes knowing your role especially challenging is that you aren't told what it is in advance or even all at once. You won't receive a confirmation letter telling you that you've found it. You have to discover it yourself, and you don't even know if and when you did. This discovery unfolds as life unfolds. Little by little, you find out what you need to know about the role you came here to play.

It is often only in looking back after possibly many decades that you understand clearly what you came here to do. This is one of the benefits of being older: You know who you are in that sense. You know the role you came to earth to play, if you haven't been sidetracked by thinking you should be living someone else's life.

On the other hand, since the life purpose is not always apparent, you may live your entire life and not be sure what your life purpose is or has been. For many, their life purpose is to learn one or more of the many basic lessons of life that contribute to being a better human being, such as becoming more compassionate, learning the joy of giving, developing one's understanding of life, or learning to be more patient or responsible. When that is the case, you may not think you have a life purpose.

Other life purposes may involve developing a talent, balancing a karmic debt, or serving others in some way, while other life purposes are things you might expect to be life purposes, since they correspond to callings or professions: fighting for civil rights, developing a new vaccine, providing products or services of some kind, or teaching or raising children.

There are many types of life purposes, and no one's life purpose is more important than another's, although some have a larger impact on the Whole than others. Each person's life purpose is as important to their soul as another's is to theirs. Furthermore, without everyone doing what they do, those with more prominent life purposes wouldn't be able to fulfill theirs.

Just as a school is designed to teach by providing a particular environment and opportunities to learn, life is designed to teach. That is the purpose of life, although not its sole purpose. Life came into being out of the pure joy of creation and to provide diverse experiences, and learning and evolution naturally followed. Learning is an inevitable byproduct of life, but it is also built into life because the Designer loves to learn and intends to do so through experiencing and creating.

Here is how learning is built into life: When you learn something useful, your ability to survive is enhanced. You are rewarded for your cleverness by improved survival, and your brain's capabilities also increase, which makes further learning more likely. You are also rewarded with pleasure. Learning is enjoyable, fun. You were designed to love learning, not only because it improves survival, but also because it is fun.

The desire to learn also ensures that you as a species will not simply survive, but also evolve, which makes life much more interesting. Learning is rewarding in that way as well and another reason it is fun. Learning makes life interesting because the resulting evolution and change is interesting. When people feel bored with life, it is often because they are not learning and evolving. That feeling of boredom is meant to point one back to learning.

A society that doesn't encourage learning or has few opportunities for it is a stagnant and unhappy one, while societies that have the freedom to learn and explore ideas naturally thrive. The greater the intellectual freedom, the greater the progress and happiness of the people. When religions discourage free thinking, intellectual thought, and exploration of a variety of ideas, they do a great disservice to their followers.

If you have a negative association with learning or school, it is not because you don't love to learn, but probably because of your experience with traditional schools and learning. Just notice, please, how much you love to learn, because this joy in learning is innate and also the silver lining in life's lessons, which are often painful and difficult.

When you hear the word "lesson," you might cringe, since lessons are often hard. But they are also interesting, and something in you also loves the challenge. Every time you are learning one of life's lessons, you are also enjoying learning it, whether you are aware of that or not. This enjoyment may be less obvious than the sense of difficulty, but it is there nonetheless.

Your true self is curious and interested in discovering what an experience is like and what can be learned from it. If you can tune in to that curiosity and love of discovery, focus on that, and accept that the rewards will come *after* the lesson, your lessons will be much easier. As in school, where you have to finish your schoolwork before you can go out to play, in the school of life, you have to learn your lesson before you can reap its benefits.

When things are difficult in the school of life, they are always followed by rewards, as long as the lesson has been learned. Life is fair that way. Although life may not always seem fair, it rewards behavior that is aligned with the Truth and withholds rewards from behavior that is not.

This may not be obvious, because human beings don't always get what they want, nor is their positive behavior always rewarded by others or their negative behavior discouraged by others. Often the opposite occurs: Bad behavior is reinforced and good behavior goes unnoticed. However, that isn't life doing that but people through their own free will. This, too, is one of life's lessons: to reinforce behaviors you wish to continue and not reinforce behaviors you do not wish to continue.

It is unfair to blame life for being unfair when it is people who are. Life is very fair, very wise, in how it shapes your behavior and teaches you. It is a very wise and compassionate teacher. Life is designed to point you to the Truth, and when you wander, it points you back to the Truth again and again if necessary.

Life is very patient and very consistent in its pointing: When you feel love, joy, and peace, you are being rewarded. When you feel the opposite, you are being encouraged to see things differently or choose differently. Even then, life allows you to choose whatever you like and experience the consequences of that. Life gives you the freedom to make good choices or not such good ones, to learn or not learn, to be happy or not.

Life does not use punishment to tell you that you are mistaken. Punishment is something human beings invented. Instead, life uses unpleasant feelings, which are (kindly) fleeting and not fatal, only uncomfortable. Negative feelings don't harm you, but they do send a message: "Something in your thinking is mistaken. Think again."

The things people might consider to be a punishment from God, such as floods, droughts, fires, earthquakes, and tidal waves, are natural occurrences and not personal. They are not a sign that you or humanity has done something wrong. God is not so indelicate. God does not behave as an angry, vengeful human might.

God is loving and nudges you gently through an inner guidance system, which includes intuitions, emotions, and more subtle feelings, such as love, joy, peace, inspiration, and excitement. You are perfectly designed to know what the

Designer is trying to teach you: When you feel happy and at peace, you are getting it. When you feel the opposite, you aren't quite getting it.

Life also teaches through consequences: If you hammer your finger instead of a nail, that will hurt. Or if you treat others badly, they are likely to treat you badly, not that this is a good choice on their part. The problem is not that life is not a good teacher, but that people are not always the best teachers, and some teach the opposite of what life is trying to teach: Some parents teach their children they can't trust themselves, some religions teach their followers that killing nonbelievers is okay, and some schools teach children lies or fail to teach them what will help them become happy. People are flawed and learning. But life is not flawed. It is perfectly designed to teach you to love.

Knowing that life is a school will help you get through challenging times. It is important that you know this so that you don't fall into the ego's trap of "This shouldn't be happening!" How much better you can feel inside if you believe that, in fact, whatever is happening *should* be happening. *Difficulties are your teacher. Whatever is happening should be happening.* That is the truth.

Notice the difference in your internal experience of these two beliefs: "This shouldn't be happening" and "This should be happening." How you feel inside is your Truth meter: If you feel relaxed and at peace, you are in the presence of the Truth. If you feel disturbed, confused, or upset, you are involved with the ego.

The problem with thinking something shouldn't be happening is that this perspective and the feelings aroused by it make it especially hard to:

❖ *Access your inner strengths and wisdom,*

❖ *Recognize the positives in the situation,*

❖ *Recognize available resources,*

❖ *Think straight and be rational,*

❖ *Enlist the help of others, and*

❖ *Learn from the challenge.*

The ego's perspective, "This shouldn't be happening," lends itself to self-pity, bitterness, anger, and a sense of victimization, which are extremely unpleasant and unfruitful states. If you feel this way, how can you possibly find the strength and wisdom to navigate your difficulty? Why make your life harder than it needs to be by clinging to a negative perspective?

Choose beliefs—even if at first you don't believe them—that help you cope and function. Override the irrational voice in your head, which tells you lies and keeps you bound by negativity and discontentment. Say no to negative thoughts, and you will discover another way of being. Moment to moment, life will show you the way to move. Life is your teacher and it is your guide. Be humble enough to let it teach and guide you.

A corollary to the perspective that difficulties are your teacher and whatever is happening should be happening is that it is not your fault that you are experiencing whatever you are experiencing. Although poor choices on your part may be responsible for some of your difficulties, no one escapes making poor choices. This is how people learn and grow. Difficulties are part of the design, including the ones caused by poor choices. Mistakes and difficulties have to be accepted and expected.

Believing that difficulties shouldn't be part of your life makes them harder to deal with than they need to be.

There is no special mantra, visualization, or secret that will eliminate difficulties from your life. No one has found one yet, although the ego is holding out hope for one. The only secret is understanding the truth about life's challenges: Your difficulties aren't personal. You are not being personally persecuted by life. Everyone experiences them. Difficulties are not proof that something is wrong with you, that you are bad, or that you are not in control of your life—no one is! As always, accepting the truth about life brings you back Home to peace and love.

Difficulties make you stronger, wiser, more patient, more careful, more responsible, and more compassionate. They change and transform you forevermore. They break your heart open, humble you, show you that you are not in control, and bring your ego to its knees. Difficulties are the primary means of evolving you, steering you in new directions, and delivering your lessons.

There are a number of reasons for these difficulties, but all serve your evolution:

1. Sometimes you bring difficulties on yourself through unwise choices, in which case you are discovering the consequences of those choices and learning to choose more wisely. "You make your bed and you lie in it." What better way to learn? Through painful experiences, you learn very quickly.

2. Other people's poor choices cause difficulties for you. These difficulties weren't necessarily intended to be your lesson, but since they landed on your doorstep, they become yours, and you inevitably learn from them. The world will

be a much kinder and easier place for everyone when fewer poor choices are made.

3. Many difficulties are ones that everyone must encounter and no one can escape: the loss of loved ones, illness, aging, and death. These experiences are profound opportunities to deepen spiritually and discover who you really are.

4. Some difficulties are designed specifically for you by your soul to steer you in a new direction or teach you something before your life can unfold further. These are times when you may be stopped in your tracks and required to reassess your life or your direction.

5. Some romantic relationships are designed specifically for your growth and not meant to be forever or ultimately fulfilling. The difficulties within these relationships are a means of working out your conditioning and preparing you for greater harmony in your future relationships. However, sometimes the lesson is simply to remove yourself from a difficult relationship. These already difficult relationships are made more challenging if you want them to be something other than they are: a means of growth.

6. Some difficulties may be karma coming to roost. Mistakes or misunderstandings carried over from previous lifetimes might be the cause of current challenges. These are some of the most important lessons and potentially some of the most difficult. These lessons usually involve others.

One of the most important ways you learn in this school of life is from the lessons that are specifically designed for you. Your soul knows exactly what you need to learn and when and how you can best learn that. There is great wisdom in how your lessons are delivered and how you are guided in learning them, although you are free to take as long as you like or to postpone learning altogether.

If you are experiencing a challenge, it is best to assume that it is related to one of these perfectly designed lessons, although you may never know if it is or what you are learning. The school of life is funny that way: You don't always know what you are learning, at least not right away. Often, though, much later you realize you have learned a thing or two. You have become wiser, more mature, more compassionate, or more easygoing. Life changes you, sometimes without you even realizing it.

Many of the lessons that have been designed for you involve others. Certain people are given to you for your growth. When this is the case, there is often a strong magnetic attraction between you, which may or may not be romantic. These relationships often feel conflicted, like you can't live with that person and you can't live without that person. These destined relationships can feel like both a blessing and a curse. When this connection is very compelling and irresistible to both, it is often a sign of karma.

Karma comes in varying degrees. Some karma defines and shapes both people's lives. When that is the case, they often end up in the same family or married to each other, and they were probably in similar relationships in other lifetimes. Other karma is brief and less serious: Someone owes you a favor, and he or she gives you something or helps you with something.

The more serious, longstanding karma is the most difficult to learn from. There are likely deep undercurrents within that relationship from other lifetimes, which are felt but not understood and which undermine harmony. Furthermore, the two people are probably very different and so naturally find it hard to get along, which was probably also true in previous lifetimes. In this lifetime, their souls have chosen to have another go at it, as they say, to learn what they failed to learn or "do over" something they did badly in another lifetime.

Karmic relationships of this nature are almost always very challenging. The learning often comes only after much suffering. Relationships where there is a lot of unhappiness, suffering, and disagreement but a commitment to stay together are likely karmic. When the lesson is learned, the individuals may move on, although they often stay together, since their difficulties have eased. What is meant to be learned varies, but such relationships are bound to significantly deepen both spiritually, since the only way out of such suffering is to surrender to love, to accept what you don't like in another.

Acceptance is one of life's most important lessons. The ego doesn't accept others but judges them and attempts to change them. Acceptance is not in the ego's repertoire because acceptance is an outgrowth of love: You naturally accept those you love. However, *if you can also accept those you don't love, you discover you can love them after all!* That is the truth, and that is the lesson. If you surrender your desire for others to be different than they are and accept the way they are, then love will flow between you.

Life also uses others to teach in more gentle ways than karma. However, contrary to what many seem to believe, not everyone you meet is there to teach you something, although you might still learn from them. With many, you are simply "ships passing in the night." Nevertheless, life uses others to teach you in many different ways: to pass on information, model behavior, inspire, deliver advice, steer you, and guide you.

The degree to which life is able to use others in this way depends on their receptivity to being used. Some are more willing instruments and more easily used than others, whether they realize they are being used or not. Those most easily used have a more developed intuition.

Those of you who are frequent instruments are likely fulfilling your life purpose in this way, at least in part. Service of some sort is many people's life purpose. When that is the case, spiritual forces will use you to convey information, teach, and guide others whom you are meant to serve, whether in a formal role of service or not.

Many are serving others informally this way. This is not a lesser life purpose than doing this more formally, as a spiritual teacher, channel, healer, or therapist, for instance. Those in the helping professions are in a position to best help others, so spiritual forces will use them to deliver messages, healing, energy, upliftment, and guidance. But let us not overlook the many who touch others every day in informal ways, in the grocery store, on social media, and in other seemingly small ways during their day.

If you feel your life purpose is to be an instrument, then ask that you become one more consciously, and you will be used more often. So much is accomplished by spiritual forces through others every day. If you only knew! You are God's hands and mouths, God's servants in so many ways. Many of you know this, although you don't have to be aware of this to be used, and most people are not.

Another way you are each other's teachers is through modeling. You are models for each other. Modeling is one of the most basic ways people learn: A mother shows her daughter how to blend the sugar into the butter when making cookies. A father shows his son how to hammer a nail. You notice *how* someone does something, and you notice *that* someone does something. Of course, you learn things that are better off not learned as well, such as smoking and swearing.

Children and people in general are masters at imitation. This is one reason advertising, television, and movies are so effective at shaping behavior. People naturally imitate what they see, especially the behavior of someone they admire or someone with more power. They will even imitate less respectable behaviors, since it is human nature to learn this way. You can't help it: "Monkey see monkey do."

The more aware you are of the power of modeling, the more choice you have around what influences you. It is especially important for parents to be aware of the impact of modeling. For instance, to think that children aren't learning to be violent by watching violence is to disregard the fact that this is exactly how people learn, whether that learning is intentional or not. Images of all kinds become part of your subconscious programming and affect your behavior without your conscious awareness or consent.

One of the most positive uses of modeling is demonstrating what is possible. People who are at the top of their game inspire others to strive for excellence: "If they can do it, so can I." You look to others for where the bar is set. Having a standard to shoot for leads to people becoming stronger and more capable, since there are always those who will try to surpass that standard. This is why each generation exceeds the last in many kinds of accomplishments.

Anyone you meet, even those who aren't acting as instruments or models, can be your teacher if you see them that way and use them that way. You can use others to discover things about yourself by simply noticing what arises inside you when you are with someone. How you automatically respond to others and the thoughts and emotions that arise in their presence show you how you have been conditioned to see yourself and others. These thoughts and emotions color your perception and shape your behavior toward others to the extent that you are unconscious of them and allow them to.

Your conditioning doesn't have to negatively affect your interactions. Simply notice the judgments, prejudices, opinions, stories, self-images, fears, and other thoughts and emotions that show up when you are with others. Notice them and then let them go and just stay present in your body and senses.

The more aware of and present you are to your own conditioning, the clearer, cleaner, and truer your interactions with others can be. The more that your conditioning is out of the way, the easier love can flow. Your egoic thoughts and emotions have never done you or others any good. They have only interfered with you being who you really are. Of course, this means you will probably talk less, but what you do say will mean more.

Choosing more consciously to learn in this way can speed your evolution exponentially. It can also be fun, and you are less likely to have to learn in more difficult ways. Some of the hardest lessons come in the form of wakeup calls, because people haven't been paying attention to what life has been trying to teach them. When you collaborate with life on learning your lessons, life gets easier.

You can even learn from people who are behaving badly toward you. Seeing other people's challenging behavior as a possible teaching can help override any tendency to react negatively toward them, which is never helpful. The perspective that you can even learn from other people's bad behavior allows you to take that behavior less personally, and that helps you be more objective and rational when dealing with them.

One of the more advanced lessons in the school of life is that other people's behavior toward you, both positive and negative, is not personal. Their behavior has more to do with their internal climate and subjective perceptions of themselves and of you than with you. Perceptions are not reality and therefore not true, and you are not responsible for other people's perceptions of you. Their perceptions belong to them. People project their ideas about you onto you, and those ideas are often not a very good match for reality.

When you realize that people's behavior toward you is not personal, their behavior loses its power to upset you. If you don't understand this, their negative behavior is likely to trigger anger, hurt feelings, or judgment in you: Anger evokes anger, hurt evokes retaliation, judgment evokes judgment. This is how the human animal responds to a threat. Once you are caught in those feelings, you lose your objectivity and ability to empathize and understand where someone is coming from. Then returning to a more rational state of mind can be an uphill battle.

If you get triggered, that is an opportunity to learn about your own conditioning, about the mistaken beliefs you still hold that can cause you to suffer. You create your internal experience, including emotions, by what you say to yourself about other people's behavior. Their behavior doesn't cause your emotions. *Other people are not powerful enough to make you angry or hurt you or make you feel any other way. You make yourself feel the way you do.* This is the truth. Seeing this is a very advanced lesson.

Getting triggered is an opportunity to see what mistaken beliefs you still hold. For instance, if someone is rude to you (which itself is a story), and you feel angry, what did you say to yourself that made you angry? Here are some possibilities: "People are so rude." "I can't believe someone would do that." "This world is a terrible place."

These are all lies because these statements are not always true. They don't tell the whole truth. People are not always rude and the world is not always a terrible place. Stop believing the lies you are telling yourself, and you won't feel angry. Learning to take responsibility for your emotions in this way will set you free from negative emotional states — yours and other people's.

Not reacting in the usual programmed way requires self-awareness, a willingness to look at your own conditioning, and understanding. The self-awareness and willingness only come with spiritual maturity. The understanding is threefold: Other people's behavior isn't personal, their behavior doesn't cause your emotions, and any bad behavior on their part is coming from their ego.

Given that bad behavior is ego-driven, people who behave badly deserve your compassion. Being caught in the ego feels terrible, and because you know how terrible it feels, you can choose not to follow them there. Instead, you can choose compassion and kindness or just remove yourself from the situation.

The willingness and ability to take the higher ground is developed by having made the automatic and less productive choice countless times and experienced the consequences. At a certain point, something in you shifts, and you see the futility of going down that same path, and you are willing to try something different.

What's left to try is kindness, compassion, acceptance, love, and understanding. You don't meet bad behavior with the same bad behavior but with love instead. Then you discover how very well that works for everyone. This is one of the most important lessons you will ever learn.

Ironically, through their negative behavior, people teach you compassion and love. They teach you that kindness is the way out of suffering, because you see that nothing else works. They don't know they are teaching you this, of course, and spiritual forces didn't specifically design this lesson for you. This lesson is for everyone, and it is built in to the school of life.

Although you are not responsible for how others perceive you, sometimes you do have something to do with their perceptions, and then there may be something to learn from their perceptions. For instance, if you have acted irresponsibly, then others may begin to perceive you as irresponsible and behave accordingly toward you or call you on this. In that case, they may be pointing out something you need to see about yourself.

Nevertheless, there is a vast difference between someone behaving irresponsibly and *being* irresponsible. No one deserves such a black and white label. No one *is* irresponsible. It simply isn't true. No one *is* anything all of the time.

What constitutes behaving irresponsibly is also debatable. *Irresponsible* is a concept and, as such, is more of a judgment than an accurate description of behavior. You did or didn't do whatever you did. Who knows what you will do in the future? Is it fair to generalize and characterize behavior, to label it, in this way?

This question is worth examining more deeply. Such labels distance people and interfere with love. They are judgments or stories. If people are judged often enough, they will become what others believe them to be. This is especially true of children. The same is true of one's beliefs about oneself: People become what they suppose themselves to be. So you are treading on shaky and dangerous ground in giving yourself and others labels. This is the egoic mind's way of maintaining the false self — yours and other people's.

Having said this, if someone, especially someone close to you, has a judgment about you, there may be some value in examining that to see if there is something within you that needs to be seen. It is likely you do have some negative tendencies because everyone does. The more aware you are of those tendencies, the more choice you have around them and the less they will run you unconsciously.

Being open to seeing these things is of great value. Others are more able to see things about you that you might not be aware of, and so their observations can be useful. Even their judgments can be useful if you can remain objective in the face of them. However, that's the problem with judgments. They don't tend to be very productive when shared because people have difficulty receiving them gracefully. Even when an insight is delivered kindly and objectively, it is often construed by one's ego as a judgment if the insight wasn't specifically asked for. It takes a lot of spiritual maturity to gracefully accept criticism from another.

Let's talk about projection. This is the psychological term for seeing something in others that is also true about yourself but denied. For instance:

❖ *When you judge someone for being a gossip, you are gossiping.*

❖ *When you see your partner as selfish, you are seeing from the eyes of your own selfish ego, which thinks your partner should be doing more for you. Who's the selfish one?*

❖ *When you are angry at someone for being unkind, you are being unkind.*

❖ *When you hate someone you think is hateful or cruel, you are experiencing that same hatred. Projecting your own hatred, greed, or ignorance onto others gives you a reason to go to war with them, and what could be more hateful, greedy, and ignorant than war?*

When you project onto others, you remain in the egoic state of consciousness, and that state is reinforced in you and perpetuated in the world. People seem to think that being aware of a negative behavior in others is proof that they, themselves, are above behaving that way. They seem to think that judging others for some behavior makes them immune to that behavior, while judgment actually makes them more susceptible to it. Judgment puts you in the same state of consciousness in which the behavior you are judging took place, making it more likely that you will do something similar.

The lesson is to see that nothing and no one is changed or healed from the egoic state of consciousness. For change and healing to take place, a shift out of that state is necessary. This is what spiritual teachings, such as mine, have long pointed to: *Love is what heals. Love is what changes hearts.* That is the truth. Judging, punishing, or rejecting others for their mistakes and failings has never helped or healed others.

What is less obvious is that judging or punishing others hurts those doing these things as much as the recipients. *It hurts you to put people out of your heart.* That is the truth. This is another more advanced lesson. Many are wise enough to see where others have gone wrong, but often their response to wrongdoing perpetuates the very state of consciousness that gave birth to that wrongdoing.

People and society will not change until they begin treating others as they would like to be treated, including those who have committed crimes. Criminals will only become more wounded if they are shunned, punished, or mistreated. Punishment cannot be the motive in dealing with those who have committed crimes. Unkindness always backfires. Violence begets violence. Only love heals and changes lives.

Lock people up if you have to, to protect society, but help them become better people. This is common sense. Everyone wins. This is another lesson—a lesson for society: Everyone is responsible for everyone else's well-being for the simple reason that their well-being affects that of society and everyone in it. You are your brother's keeper. If you shirk this responsibility, it is you who will suffer. "Do unto others as you would have them do unto you" makes everyone happy.

CHAPTER 7

The Truth About Emotions

I want to tell you the truth about emotions, since there are some misunderstandings about them. Emotions do provide some information, and for that they are useful. Later in this chapter, I will explain just what kind of useful information emotions do provide. But first, let's clear up some of the misconceptions.

The problem is that people think their emotions tell them something true and useful about themselves and others, while feelings don't actually inform you about objective reality. For instance, people often say things like, "I feel lost" or "I feel alone." Having such feelings makes them believe they *are* actually lost or alone, when there is no evidence for that. Feelings make something seem true that is not true. In other words, your feelings aren't true! They don't tell the truth.

Here are some more examples of how people mistakenly assume that their emotions give them objective feedback about reality:

❖ *When people are angry, they think that means someone wronged them or someone was in the wrong. Their anger is their barometer of the morality of the behavior going on around them: A car crosses in front of them, and their anger is proof to them that the car shouldn't have done that.*

❖ *When people feel afraid, they think that means there is a real threat.*

❖ *When people are sad, they think that means something went wrong, something happened that shouldn't have happened.*

Emotions cause you to believe things that aren't true. Emotions lie. All they do is tell you about what is going on inside of you, not outside of you. They belong to your personal, subjective reality, the illusory reality of the self you believe yourself to be. Feelings justify the ego or imaginary self's *perceptions* of reality, but they don't actually represent reality. They belong to the illusory reality, which reinforces and sustains the false beliefs of the false self and keeps you from seeing reality as it actually is. Emotions color and distort reality.

This reliance on emotions as indicators of what is true about a situation is often supported by psychotherapists in their focus on emotions and "honoring" them. Although there is value in uncovering and examining emotions, as will be explained shortly, I'm going to play devil's advocate for a moment and present a more unorthodox perspective on emotions.

One of the tasks of therapy is to uncover emotions that have been buried in the unconscious mind. We can all agree that this is helpful, as repressed emotions are problematic. They burst forth at inopportune moments and fuel many acts of violence. Repressed emotions are also behind anxiety, depression, and addictions, including food addictions and other compulsive behaviors. So it is admirable to want to do something about repressed emotions.

The obvious thing to do is to bring buried emotions to the surface, acknowledge them, and "honor them." However, this is where things can take an unhealthy and unhelpful turn. Rather than defusing and healing emotions, much of the exploration of emotions done in psychotherapy only keeps them around, except now they are more conscious.

One of the goals of psychotherapy is to discover why someone feels angry, unhappy, and unworthy. Therapy seeks justification in events for people's emotions. What is generally discovered is that abuse, neglect, or trauma in one's early life is behind any negative emotions. That understanding helps people feel better and supported. They see that they have a good reason for feeling the way they do. They see that their feelings aren't wrong after all and that they aren't bad for having feelings. In this way, therapy offers some relief.

Unfortunately, uncovering events that explain why people feel the way they do and helping them feel okay about those feelings only gives those emotions legitimacy. It "honors" those feelings, but it doesn't heal them or release people from them.

There is nothing wrong, of course, with emotions or with uncovering the source of one's feelings. Nevertheless, the attitude that feelings should be honored is misguided. That is like honoring a lie, when what is needed is to see that those emotions are based on a lie, on a false or incorrect conclusion.

Children are especially prone to forming incorrect conclusions about their experiences because they don't have an adult's perspective, understanding, or coping skills. For that reason, most emotional wounding happens in childhood. Invariably, children blame themselves for their parents' abuse and mistakes. Unfortunately, with children, this is how it is.

Adults would not come to those same conclusions because they have a better understanding of life.

A child's painful emotions are often repressed because they are so overwhelming and frightening. What makes them that way are the mistaken conclusions the child came to, however unconscious those conclusions may have been: "The people I'm dependent on for my survival don't love me. I must be unlovable. I must be a terrible, bad person. I might not survive."

These unconscious conclusions cause unbearable and unmanageable emotions, which the child's psyche represses as a protective mechanism to keep from feeling those emotions. However, as long as such conclusions remain unconscious, they will continue to define one's identity and shape one's behavior.

So people are stuck with how their young ego saw the incidents of the past and saw themselves, and that becomes their ego's truth and their identity: "I'm unlovable. I'll never be happy. No one can be trusted." The meaning they gave to what happened to them hurt them on top of the actual abuse or neglect. Their unbearable feelings added insult to injury. The past is over, but the painful conclusions still affect their life and well-being.

When psychotherapy focuses on how bad the childhood circumstances were, it justifies these intense emotions. Therapy agrees with victims that they have good cause to feel the way they do, which is not untrue. However, the real work in therapy is to uncover the conclusions that contributed to the child's pain, many of which are unconscious, and to help one arrive at other, truer and more positive conclusions.

Although people are stuck with what happened in the past, since the past cannot be changed, they don't have to be stuck with their conclusions about the past. People can come to see their past differently, in a way that doesn't leave them feeling angry, hurt, or unworthy. Reformulating their mistaken conclusions frees people from emotions related to the past. This reformulation is called reframing: What happened is seen from a larger perspective, put in a larger frame.

Healing emotions is a matter of correcting the conclusions that continue to affect one's life, not analyzing the past or dwelling on it by retelling it, which only keeps the emotional pain alive. Uncovering the events behind painful emotions doesn't change the past or the emotions and too often becomes a justification for those emotions rather than a means for healing them and becoming free from them.

How is having a justification for your emotions helpful? Won't you just continue to try to justify your feelings going forward: "Of course I'm angry. He shouldn't have done that to me!" Instead of repressing or suppressing your anger, as you might have done in the past, you will be proud of it: "I'm just expressing my anger. What's wrong with that?" After all, you learned that repressing your emotions wasn't healthy. Or instead of repressing your sadness, you will "honor" it by wallowing in it and turning it into an identity: "Of course I'm sad. I had a sad life. That's who I am. That's how it is."

With your emotions front and center and the belief that they are true and meaningful, it is a short trip to justifying hurtful and unhealthy actions. If your feelings are justified, then why wouldn't behavior that follows from them be justified as well? If you are living in an emotionally-laden inner world because you see feelings as true, important, and justified, then they are bound to lead you astray and cause you to act in ways you later regret.

If you feel that your emotions justify your actions, then why does it matter what religion or society says? So the result of "honoring" feelings is often that emotions override morality, and people feel comfortable meting out punishment based on their emotions. Their feelings seem true and righteous, so actions stemming from them must be as well, or so it is reasoned.

Is this not the justification for terrorism and war? You have been harmed (or you might be), and the hatred, anger, and hurt that result justify retaliating in harmful ways. In this way, war always appears just, and so it continues. This attitude is even reflected in society. Even though society prohibits victims from meting out their own justice, the justice system exacts revenge in its own way through the penal system, which is indeed penalizing.

People go around and around in their feeling-fueled reality, suffering and causing others to suffer, without realizing that the suffering can stop — but only if the truth about feelings and about life is understood. So here is the truth: *Emotions belong to the ego and uphold the ego's illusory reality. They do not deserve honoring, but they do deserve investigation.* To clarify this statement, we need to distinguish between emotions, which come from the ego, and more subtle, truer feelings, such as love, which by this definition is not an emotion.

Everyone knows when they are experiencing an emotion because it is accompanied by certain physical reactions: Your face flushes or become pale, your heart beats faster, you become hot or cold, you sweat, you become tense, or you feel sick or like you've been punched in the gut. Every emotion has its own signature in the body.

What I am calling emotions are feelings that stem from egoic thoughts, which one may or may not be conscious of. These emotions leave you feeling either uncomfortable or off-balance. Undesirable emotions, such as sadness and anger, feel uncomfortable, if not much worse. And more desirable emotions, such as excitement and happiness, make you feel off-balance. Although you may want to feel happy and excited all the time, that isn't how it works. What goes up must come down. No matter what the emotion, positive or negative, if an emotion is present, peace and equanimity are not. Emotions stir you up and sap your energy. They take you on a rollercoaster ride of ups and downs, highs and lows.

What I am calling truer feelings, which are often confused with emotions, do not come from egoic thoughts and do not stir you up or sap your energy. Truer feelings are the subtle experience of the true self as it manifests in life. They are what I have been referring to as qualities of the Truth, such as peace, love, gratitude, and compassion.

These truer feelings are not e-motions because they don't set you in motion. Instead, they are more of an absence of motion, since they come from the stillness of your true self. When you are in touch with peace, love, gratitude, compassion, strength, or any other quality of your true nature, you experience a solidity and equanimity that does not exist in the egoic state of consciousness, especially when emotions are present.

Discriminating between emotions and the subtler feelings of your true nature is simple. Emotions feel unsettling and most are unpleasant. You feel you have to do something about them. On the other hand, feelings from your deeper self are settling and always pleasant: Nothing is missing, there is no problem, all is well.

The thoughts in the egoic state of consciousness that produce emotions may be so quiet or so little in your awareness that you don't realize they are responsible for what you are feeling—until you take a look. This is where investigation comes in. By becoming aware of an emotion and then investigating the thoughts behind it, you can become free of that emotion. Investigation defuses and can eventually eliminate negative emotions or at least minimize their effect in your life.

Did you know you have the power to master your emotions, not just control them? Imagine what a different world this would be if the only emotions that remained were not compelling or "true" enough to cause people to act on them? This is what an enlightened society would be like: no more anger or hatred to repress, suppress, act out, or even express. If an emotion arose, it would be seen for what it is, and that would be enough to defuse it. Many are living this way even today.

There is a way to relate to emotions that is not acting them out, repressing them, or even expressing them. The alternative is to be with the emotion and investigate it in the following way:

❖ *Notice the emotion.*

❖ *Accept that it is there (because it is).*

❖ *Let it be there, and let yourself experience it.*

❖ *Sit with the emotion with curiosity and invite it to reveal the beliefs behind it.*

❖ *See that those beliefs are untrue.*

Once you are aware of an emotion, you can work backwards from that emotion and discover the thought or thoughts that caused it. When you choose to investigate an emotion in this way, you have turned the tables on it: That emotion is no longer controlling you; you are using it to uncover the mistaken beliefs that underpin the Illusion.

Emotions provide very useful information. Although they don't tell you what is objectively true, they do tell you what you believe to be true but which is not altogether true. Emotions show you the false beliefs, generalizations, misunderstandings, stories, assumptions, judgments, and black-and-white thinking that uphold the ego's illusory reality and the imaginary you that exists in that reality. By investigating your emotions, you can begin to disassemble your ego's illusory reality and the false self. Then what is left is your true self and life the way it really is.

Once you understand the truth about emotions, you are empowered to free yourself from the ego's lies. Every undesirable emotion points to a lie that helps uphold the ego's reality. The fastest way to dismantle the ego's reality is to examine your emotions and discover what is really going on. Here is what you can discover:

Anger comes from unmet expectations. Expectations are fabricated assumptions about how life should be and what should happen. Since expectations are made up, they are not true. They are part of the ego's imaginary reality: what it wants and hopes life to be, not the way things actually are.

Sadness comes from an assumption that something shouldn't have happened. Who says it shouldn't have happened if it did? The ego declares that something shouldn't have happened because it doesn't accept the way life is, but that declaration doesn't change the way it is. Refusing to accept reality causes the suffering that is so prevalent in the egoic state of consciousness. Assumptions are examples of the ego's wishful thinking.

Fear comes from a negative belief about the future. But the future does not exist. It is made up, so any beliefs about it are made up as well. Fear is an important part of the ego's imaginary reality because fear is so convincing. It convinces you that the ego's beliefs and perceptions are real. Fear keeps you in the imaginary reality and out of touch with the Truth.

Shame comes from a belief in inadequacy, and inadequacy is a concept. As useful and necessary as concepts are in communicating with others, concepts are mental constructs and not part of objective reality. There is no such thing as inadequacy. Shame, like all feelings, is something real that comes from something unreal, an imagination or a belief. This is why feelings are so convincing. Your real feelings convince you of something that is not real or not true.

Regret comes from the mistaken belief that something could have been different, when things could only have been as they were. "Could," in referring to the past, is always a lie. "Could" is a useless and untrue supposition about the past.

Jealousy and *envy* come from the mistaken belief that someone is better or less than someone else. Better than and less than are concepts, which have no value or validity in relation to human beings. They are imaginary and untrue measuring sticks. Everyone is equally cherished and precious.

Hatred comes from believing the ego's judgments and negative stories about others, which are never the whole story. The ego builds a case against others by seeing only the negative and also by defining something as negative. It naturally fears and distrusts others because they are different. To the ego, being different is bad and a reason to hate them. The ego does not see the Truth, which is *love and Oneness, and so it is left with its judgments, hatred, and fear.*

Here is an example of what you might discover when you investigate an emotion. Let's suppose you are upset about something someone said to you. They criticized you, and you feel hurt and angry. If you sit with those feelings with acceptance, curiosity, and receptivity and make space for your intuition to reveal the truth about them, you will discover a number of things.

First of all, you can discover that you created that hurt and anger, not someone else, by believing what that person said. Otherwise, you would have no reason to feel hurt and angry. Something in your subjective reality agreed with that person's subjective reality, or the criticism would have had no effect. Other people can't actually hurt you or make you angry unless you buy in to their thoughts or buy in to your own thoughts.

Is what that person said actually true? Maybe there is some truth to it that is worth examining. But if what that person said triggered negative emotions in you, most likely it is their ego's truth. It came from that person's subjective reality and was probably some form of judgment designed to confirm that person's subjective reality and put that person on top. This is what egos do. If you buy in to another person's ego's reality, you will probably get caught up in your own ego's reality, although it is possible to see that this is going on and not do that.

If that level of investigation doesn't get you beyond the hurt and anger, then you can explore what thoughts in your own subjective reality hooked you. What do you believe about yourself that made you feel hurt and angry? Or what other beliefs do you have that made you feel hurt and angry? It could be any number of beliefs:

> *He doesn't like me.*
> *People never like me.*
> *No one understands me.*
> *I never do anything right.*
> *He sees how inadequate I am.*
> *He shouldn't talk to me that way.*
> *How dare he think that!*
> *He is so stupid.*
> *I can't stand people like him.*
> *He's such a jerk.*

None of these thoughts is useful or completely true. This is what needs to be seen in investigating your thoughts. The thoughts that make you feel hurt, sad, angry, fearful, hateful, jealous, regretful, or ashamed are not the whole truth. Most are gross generalizations, exaggerations, and assumptions, and all fuel emotions you don't want to have.

So why do people do this to themselves? Why do they believe their minds? They really don't have a choice until they realize what is going on — that *thoughts and feelings don't tell the truth.* Until you realize this great truth, you are stuck with the lies and suffering of the egoic state of consciousness. You will see life through the lens of your ego, and you will miss the beauty, peace, love, and bounty of the life you are given.

Emotions cause the suffering that eventually motivates people to find a way out of their subjective reality and suffering. So you could say that even emotions are pointers to the Truth. Sadness or unhappiness and particularly depression, because of the degree of suffering involved, often are very effective in getting people to question more deeply. Nevertheless, emotions are not one of the ways the true self communicates with you. For instance, your true self does not use fearful thoughts to warn you about some future event. Emotions are there to hold the Illusion in place, not to provide any useful or true information.

Depression is a sign that one is deeply believing the ego's perceptions. Depression is extremely painful, and interventions are often necessary when someone has fallen that far into the darkness of negativity. To bring back a more balanced perspective, drugs are often helpful and necessary.

What happens is that negative nonphysical forces can and do aggravate the negativity of one's ego and cause that negativity to be so compelling that one feels powerless to do anything about it. A clearing of that negative energy is necessary, and help should be sought from healers and others capable of working with negative entities and negative thoughts.

A lack of alignment with one's soul's plan is what is likely to have gotten one into trouble in the first place. When people don't allow themselves to follow their Heart, they often create a life unsuited to them and one that can never make them happy. Depression is often an indicator that someone has reached a dead end and needs to make significant changes. If those changes aren't made, one becomes increasingly vulnerable to further psychic attack and manipulation by negative forces. People can go very far down the rabbit hole of negativity and be unable to pull themselves out.

It is so important that you align with what makes your Heart sing and your energy light up. Life is hard enough without the challenge of being out of sync with your soul's plan. Anyone can be happy and fulfilled, but you have to be willing to do what makes you happy on the deepest level. Are you willing to do whatever it takes to find happiness, not the usual kind of happiness, but a happiness that is imperturbable and founded on love?

Love is your true nature, and it is by loving that you find your way, by going after what you love and by responding to life with love and acceptance. Grace delivers its lessons and its gifts, and by being willing to learn those lessons and receive those gifts, you find your way Home. Grace is the great goodness behind all life, and it carries you on wings of love every step of the way. Know this, and your way will be made clear.

The Truth About Life

1. You are life, and you are infinite!

2. You are not in control of life, and you don't need to be because your infinite self is.

3. The intelligence behind life has a design.

4. The Designer and the design are good. Life is good!

5. You don't know very much for certain — and you don't need to know.

6. When you don't accept the way life is, you suffer.

7. Life is a school. Your experiences are your teachers. You are here to learn and grow.

8. The only thing in life that is black and white are those colors. There is a positive side to every negative experience and vice versa.

9. Everything is unfolding as it needs to.

10. Whatever is happening is what life in your corner of the universe is all about for you for now.

11. You always have whatever you need to deal with whatever life brings you.

12. Everyone is learning from everyone else. Everyone is learning, and everyone is teaching.

13. Difficulties are your teacher. Whatever is happening should be happening.

14. Love is what heals. Love is what changes hearts.

15. If you can accept those you don't love, you discover you can love them after all! If you surrender your desire for others to be different than they are, then love will flow between you.

16. Other people are not powerful enough to make you angry or hurt you or make you feel any other way. You make yourself feel the way you do.

17. It hurts you to put people out of your heart.

18. Emotions belong to the ego and uphold the ego's illusory reality. They do not deserve honoring, but they do deserve investigation.

19. Thoughts and feelings don't tell the truth.

ABOUT the AUTHOR

Gina Lake is a spiritual teacher and the author of numerous books about awakening to one's true nature, including *The Jesus Trilogy, In the World but Not of It, A Heroic Life, From Stress to Stillness, Trusting Life, Embracing the Now, Radical Happiness, Living in the Now, Ten Teachings for One World, Return to Essence, Choosing Love, Anatomy of Desire,* and *Getting Free.* She is also a gifted intuitive with a master's degree in counseling psychology and over twenty-five years' experience supporting people in their spiritual growth. Her website offers information about her books and online courses, free e-books, book excerpts, a blog, a monthly newsletter, and audio and video recordings:

www.radicalhappiness.com

If you enjoyed this book, we think you will also enjoy these other books from Jesus by Gina Lake...

Jesus Speaking: On Falling in Love with Life: This audiobook is Jesus speaking from another dimension today. His message, as channeled through Gina Lake, is meant to bring you into greater alignment with the Christ within you, with Christ Consciousness. It is also intended to give you the experience of having a relationship with the wise and gentle being we've known as Jesus the Christ, as he speaks to you as if you were sitting in his presence. In it, you will discover how to become the loving, strong, and peaceful being you are meant to be, which Jesus exemplified. 5 hours.

Available only at:

www.RadicalHappiness.com/audio-video/jesus-channelings

In the World but Not of It: New Teachings from Jesus on Embodying the Divine: From the Introduction, by Jesus: "What I have come to teach now is that you can embody love, as I did. You can become Christ within this human life and learn to embody all that is good within you. I came to show you the beauty of your own soul and what is possible as a human. I came to show you that it is possible to be both human and divine, to be love incarnate. You are equally both. You walk with one foot in the world of form and another in the Formless. This mysterious duality within your being is what this book is about." This book is another in a series of books dictated to Gina Lake by Jesus.

The Radical Happiness Online Course

Meditation will change your life because meditation changes your brain like nothing else can. Find out how. Get serious about waking up and becoming happier. The Radical Happiness online course will show you how and get you started. This 8-week course, which can be begun anytime, will provide you with a foundation for awakening and increase your happiness through spiritual practices, a structure for doing those practices, and support from an online forum. This course uses a combination of written text, instructional audios, guided meditations, inquiries, and exercises. The practices include four types of meditation, spiritual inquiry, breathing practices, a gratitude practice, love and forgiveness practices, prayer, and others. For more information, please visit:

www.RadicalHappiness.com/courses

More Books by Gina Lake

Available in paperback, ebook, and audiobook formats.

The Jesus Trilogy. In this trilogy by Jesus, are three jewels, each shining in its own way and illuminating the same truth: You are not only human but divine, and you are meant to flourish and love one another. In words that are for today, Jesus speaks intimately and directly to the reader of the secrets to peace, love, and happiness. He explains the deepest of all mysteries: who you are and how you can live as he taught long ago. The three books in *The Jesus Trilogy* were dictated to Gina Lake by Jesus and include *Choice and Will, Love and Surrender,* and *Beliefs, Emotions, and the Creation of Reality.*

A Heroic Life: New Teachings from Jesus on the Human Journey. The hero's journey—this human life—is a search for the greatest treasure of all: the gifts of your true nature. These gifts are your birthright, but they have been hidden from you, kept from you by the dragon: the ego. These gifts are the wisdom, love, peace, courage, strength, and joy that reside at your core. *A Heroic Life* shows you how to overcome the ego's false beliefs and face the ego's fears. It provides you with both a perspective and a map to help you successfully and happily navigate life's challenges and live heroically. This book is another in a series of books dictated to Gina Lake by Jesus.

From Stress to Stillness: Tools for Inner Peace. Most stress is created by how we think about things. *From Stress to Stillness* will help you to examine what you are thinking and change your relationship to your thoughts so that they no longer result in stress. Drawing from the wisdom traditions, psychology, New Thought, and the author's own experience as a spiritual teacher and counselor, *From Stress to Stillness* offers many practices and suggestions that will lead to greater peace and equanimity, even in a busy and stress-filled world.

Embracing the Now: Finding Peace and Happiness in What Is. The Now—this moment—is the true source of happiness and peace and the key to living a fulfilled and meaningful life. *Embracing the Now* is a collection of essays that can serve as daily reminders of the deepest truths. Full of clear insight and wisdom, *Embracing the Now* explains how the mind keeps us from being in the moment, how to move into the Now and stay there, and what living from the Now is like. It also explains how to overcome stumbling blocks to being in the Now, such as fears, doubts, misunderstandings, judgments, distrust of life, desires, and other conditioned ideas that are behind human suffering.

Radical Happiness: A Guide to Awakening provides the keys to experiencing the happiness that is ever-present and not dependent on circumstances. This happiness comes from realizing that who you think you are is not who you really are. *Radical Happiness* describes the nature of the egoic state of consciousness and how it interferes with happiness, what awakening and enlightenment are, and how to live in the world after awakening.

Living in the Now: How to Live as the Spiritual Being That You Are. The 99 essays in *Living in the Now* will help you realize your true nature and live as that. They answer many questions raised by the spiritual search and offer wisdom on subjects such as fear, anger, happiness, aging, boredom, desire, patience, forgiveness, acceptance, love, commitment, meditation, being present, emotions, trusting your Heart, and many other deep subjects. These essays will help you become more conscious, present, happy, loving, grateful, at peace, and fulfilled.

Return to Essence: How to Be in the Flow and Fulfill Your Life's Purpose describes how to get into the flow and stay there and how to live life from there. Being in the flow and not being in the flow are two very different states. One is dominated by the ego-driven mind, which is the cause of suffering, while the other is the domain of Essence, the Divine within each of us. You are meant to live in the flow. The flow is the experience of Essence—your true self—as it lives life through you and fulfills its purpose for this life.

Anatomy of Desire: How to Be Happy Even When You Don't Get What You Want will help you discriminate between your Heart's desires and the ego's. It will help you be happy regardless of your desires and whether you are attaining them. So *Anatomy of Desire* is also about spiritual freedom, or liberation, which comes from following the Heart, our deepest desires, instead of the ego's desires. It is about becoming a lover of life rather than a desirer.

Getting Free: How to Move Beyond Conditioning and Be Happy. To a large extent, healing our conditioning involves changing our relationship to our mind and discovering who we really are. *Getting Free* will help you do that. It will also help you reprogram your mind; clear negative thoughts and self-images; use meditation, prayer, forgiveness, and gratitude; work with spiritual forces to assist healing and clear negativity; and heal entrenched issues from the past.

Choosing Love: Moving from Ego to Essence in Relationships. Having a truly meaningful relationship requires choosing love over your conditioning, that is, your ideas, fantasies, desires, images, and beliefs. *Choosing Love* describes how to move beyond conditioning, judgment, anger, romantic illusions, and differences to the experience of love and oneness with another. It explains how to drop into the core of your Being, where Oneness and love exist, and be with others from there.

Trusting Life: Overcoming the Fear and Beliefs That Block Peace and Happiness. Fear and distrust keep us from living the life we were meant to live, and they are the greatest hurdles to seeing the truth about life—that it is good, abundant, supportive, and potentially joyous. *Trusting Life* is a deep exploration into the mystery of who we are, why we suffer, why we don't trust life, and how to become more trusting. It offers tools for overcoming the fear and beliefs that keep us from falling in love with life.

For more information, please visit the "Books" page at

www.RadicalHappiness.com

20792516R00093

Printed in Great Britain
by Amazon